The Puritans on the Providence of God

by
Edward Corbet
William Pemble
William Gouge
with chapters by C. Matthew McMahon

Copyright Information

The Puritans on the Providence of God, by Edward Corbet, William Pemble and William Gouge, with chapters by C. Matthew McMahon
Edited by Therese B. McMahon

© 2025 by Puritan Publications and A Puritan's Mind

Published by Puritan Publications
A Ministry of A Puritan's Mind®
Crossville, TN: Puritan Publications, 2025
www.puritanpublications.com
www.apuritansmind.com
www.gracechapeltn.com
www.reformedsynod.com

All rights reserved. No part of this publication may be reproduced, stored in a retrieval system or transmitted in any form by any means, electronic, mechanical, photocopy, recording or otherwise, without the prior permission of the publisher, except as provided by USA copyright law.

First Electronic Edition 2025
First Modern Print Edition 2025
Manufactured in the United States of America

eISBN: 978-1-62663-504-3
ISBN: 978-1-62663-505-0

Table of Contents

Edward Corbet: A Faithful Minister.............................4

William Pemble: A Short Life, A Godly Legacy 9

William Gouge: A Life of Faithful Labor and Piety . 14

The Providence of God: Christ's Sovereign Hand in All Things 21

TREATISE 1: God's Providence Over All Things......28

TREATISE 2: The Providence of God 64

TREATISE 3: The Progress of Divine Providence ... 99

Other Works Published by Puritan Publications ...151

Edward Corbet: A Faithful Minister
by C. Matthew McMahon, Ph.D., Th.D.

Edward Corbet (d. 1658), Westminster Divine, though not a household name among the great Puritans, left a legacy that speaks to the faithfulness of God's providence in raising up men for His glory. Born in Pontesbury, Shropshire, Corbet hailed from the ancient and respectable family of the *Corbets* in that county. His early education at Shrewsbury and later at Merton College, Oxford, prepared him for a life of scholarship and ministry.

At Merton, Corbet demonstrated a precocious mind, earning his B.A. on December 4, 1622, and distinguishing himself as a probationer fellow in 1624. His academic achievements were matched only by his unflinching resistance to the innovations of Archbishop Laud, a stand that would later earn him a role in Laud's trial. Corbet's reputation as a defender of Reformed orthodoxy was well-established, and his unwavering commitment to Scripture and the purity of worship marked him as one "always puritannically affected."

A Preacher Before Parliament

Corbet's most significant public contribution came in his role as a preacher to the Long Parliament. On December 28, 1642, he delivered a sermon based on 1 Corinthians 1:27, entitled *God's Providence* (part of this current volume). Preached during a solemn fast before the House of Commons, this discourse remains his only surviving manuscript. The sermon, which reflected Corbet's depth of theological understanding and conviction, received the thanks of the House and led to his appointment as rector of Chartham, Kent, by parliamentary ordinance on May 17, 1643.

During his time at Chartham, Corbet faithfully ministered to his flock, embodying the Puritan ideal of a shepherd who diligently feeds the sheep of Christ. However, his tenure there was cut short in 1646 when he returned to Oxford. Parliament appointed him as one of seven ministers tasked with bringing the loyal scholars of the university into submission—a role he found burdensome and contrary to his disposition.

Scholar, Pastor, and Family Man

Despite the political turbulence of his era, Corbet continued to labor for the gospel. In 1647, he was installed as public minister and canon of Christ Church, succeeding Dr. Henry Hammond, who had been ejected. Yet, true to his character as "a person of conscience and honesty," Corbet resigned both positions the following year. His academic journey culminated in his Doctor of Divinity degree, conferred on April 12, 1648.

In the beginning of 1649, Corbet was presented with the rectory of Great Hasely, near Oxford, where he served until his death. This position allowed him to focus on pastoral ministry and the care of his parishioners. Corbet's personal life was marked by devotion to his family. He married Margaret Brent, daughter of Sir Nathaniel Brent, with whom he had three children—Edward, Martha, and Margaret. His wife's death in 1656 deeply affected him, but Corbet remained steadfast in his calling until the Lord called him home on January 5, 1658.

A Legacy of Scholarship and Piety

Corbet's contributions extended beyond the pulpit. His generosity and love for knowledge are evidenced in his will, which bequeathed Bishop Robert Abbot's *Commentaries on the Romans*—a four-volume manuscript—to the public library of Oxford University.

His gift of books to Shrewsbury and Merton further demonstrated his commitment to the advancement of godly learning.

Though only his sermon *God's Providence* seems to have survived, its themes resonate deeply with the biblical and reformed understanding of divine sovereignty. Preaching on God's choice of the "foolish things" to confound the wise, Corbet emphasized the inscrutable and awe-inspiring nature of God's providence. His life, marked by humble service and unwavering faith, stands as a testament to the doctrine he proclaimed.

Corbet's role in the Westminster Assembly of Divines and his witness against Laud's innovations underscore his place among the Reformed faithful. Yet, it is his quiet, consistent labors as a pastor and scholar that truly define his legacy. He was not a man who sought fame but one who sought faithfulness—a hallmark of Puritan ministry.

The Lesson of Providence

Edward Corbet's story reminds us of the wisdom of God's providence in raising up men for His purposes, often in ways the world cannot comprehend. In a time of political and religious upheaval, Corbet stood firm as a shepherd of souls and a steward of God's truth. His life, though cut short at fifty-five years, bore fruit that continues to encourage believers to trust in the sovereign hand of God.

As we consider the life of this faithful minister, may we be stirred to greater confidence in the providence of God, who, "worketh all things after the counsel of His own will," (Ephesians 1:11).

William Pemble: A Short Life, A Godly Legacy
by C. Matthew McMahon, Ph.D., Th.D.

"Here lieth the Body of William Pemble, Master of Arts and Preacher, who died April 14, 1623."
— *Inscription* on his grave.

William Pemble (1591–1623), though young in years, was a towering figure of godly scholarship, a Puritan divine of exceptional learning and piety. Born the son of a minister in Egerton, Kent, he grew up immersed in the Scriptures, nourished in the school of Christ from his earliest days. Educated at Magdalen College, Oxford, under the tutelage of Mr. Richard Capel[1]—a man equally devoted to Reformed truth—Pemble's mind and heart were shaped by both the

---

[1] Puritan Publications has republished one of Capel's most famous works, *The Nature, Danger and Cure of Temptation*.

discipline of academic rigor and the sanctifying hand of God's grace.

It was said of Pemble (though young) that, "he attained a high degree of heavenly wisdom," not merely through the usual means of study but by weathering affliction and temptation with unwavering faith. His biography testifies that, even as a young man, he offered to God a sacrifice of *service* and *holiness* surpassing that of many older and more seasoned brethren.

At the university, his reputation was unmatched. In the halls of Magdalen College, Pemble became a celebrated preacher and an intellectual light. His accomplishments were manifold: "a zealous Calvinist, a famous preacher, an excellent artist, a skillful linguist, a good orator, an expert mathematician, and an ornament to the society to which he belonged." Such was the testimony of those who knew him. Adrian Heereboord, the renowned professor of philosophy at Leyden, lavished praise upon his works, while another writer marveled that Pemble had, "thoroughly traced the circle of the arts" and reached a pinnacle of mastery in both the sciences and the loftiest realms of theological reflection. Magdalen College, in those days, was rightly called a nursery of Puritanism, a fertile ground for training reformers who sought both doctrinal precision and personal holiness. Pemble stood among their number, though he did not press his nonconformity as far as some of his brethren. His heart burned for the reformation of the Church, advocating the relaxation of rigid subscription and other points of conformity. Yet, it was not just his own labors that left a mark. As a tutor, Pemble shaped the minds and hearts of many Puritan luminaries who went on to serve with distinction in the cause of Christ.

Let it not be said, as some have falsely claimed, that the Puritans were unlearned. Pemble's life is a sufficient rebuttal. He demonstrated that fidelity to Reformed doctrine did not preclude, but rather demanded, the highest levels of scholarship and intellectual engagement.

It was during a visit to his former tutor, Mr. Capel, now minister at Eastington in Gloucestershire, that Pemble's earthly pilgrimage came to an abrupt end. Falling ill, he passed into glory at the tender age of thirty-two. His body was laid to rest in Eastington's churchyard, beneath a humble yet eloquent inscription. His legacy, however, was anything but small.

In life, Pemble preached the righteousness of Christ with fervor. In death, he clung to that same truth with unwavering confidence. He departed, "in the comfortable and full persuasion of justification by faith in the righteousness of Jesus Christ." And what of his sermons? Even Bishop Wilkins, in his catalog of the finest preaching of that age, included Pemble's name—a fitting testimony to the lasting value of his ministry.

William Pemble, though his years were few, lived a life that glorified the Savior in scholarship, service, and steadfastness. His works and witness remain, calling us to treasure Christ above all and to labor faithfully in the fields of His Kingdom.

His Works:
1. A Treatise of Justification by Faith, 1625.
2. A Treatise of Providence.
3. The Book of Ecclesiastes Explained, 1628.
4. A Plea for Grace, more especially the Grace of Faith, 1629.
5. An Exposition of the first Nine Chapters of Zechariah, 1629.
6. Five godly and profitable Sermons, 1629.
7. Fruitful Sermons on 1 Cor. xv. 18, 19., 1629.
8. An Introduction to the Worthy Receiving of the Lord's Supper, 1629.
9. De formarum originc, 1629.
10. De Senibus interim, 1629.
11. A Sum of Moral Philosophy, 1630.
12. The period of the Persian monarchie Wherein sundry places of Ezra, Nehemiah and Daniel are cleered: extracted, contracted, and englished, much of it out of Doctor Raynolds, by the late learned and godly man William Pemble, of Magdalen Hall in Oxford. Published and enlarged since his death by his friend, Richard Capel., 1631.
13. Enchiridion Oratorium, 1633.
14. An Introduction to Geography, 1685.

The above works in English were collected and published in one volume folio, 1635, being *much* esteemed and often reprinted.

William Gouge: A Life of Faithful Labor and Piety
by C. Matthew McMahon, Ph.D., Th.D.

"Them that honour me will I honour," (1 Samuel 2:30).

William Gouge (1575–1653), Westminster Divine, a towering figure of Reformed piety and learning, was born in Stratford, Bow, Middlesex, on November 1, 1575. From the start, Gouge's life was marked by the providence of God. His family tree read like a who's who of Puritan excellence—his mother, daughter of the esteemed merchant Nicholas Culverel, was sister to the preachers Samuel and Ezekiel Culverel. Two of her sisters were married to giants of the faith: Dr. Chadderton, master of Emmanuel College, and Dr. Whitaker, professor of divinity at Cambridge.

Gouge's early education at St. Paul's School and Felstead Free School set him on a trajectory of scholarly and spiritual excellence. Under the ministry of his uncle Ezekiel Culverel, he grew deeply in faith, and from his time at Eton College, he displayed an unusual seriousness. While his peers pursued recreation, Gouge delighted in study and prayer, cultivating a reverence for God and a distaste for the profanation of the Sabbath, which was then widespread.

At King's College, Cambridge, Gouge's brilliance was evident. A devoted student of *Ramus*' logic[2] and a skilled debater, he defended truth with precision and zeal. Rising early for prayer and Bible reading, he disciplined himself to read fifteen chapters of Scripture daily, a practice he maintained throughout his life. His mastery of Hebrew began under a Jewish tutor, and his dedication to study made him a sought-after mentor to others.

Though he wished to remain at Cambridge, his father arranged a marriage that ultimately served the church. At thirty-two, Gouge began his pastoral ministry, entering the pulpit with knowledge and maturity. For over 45 years, he served as the minister of Blackfriars, London, faithfully shepherding his flock and laboring for their spiritual growth.

Shepherd of Blackfriars

---

[2] *Peter Ramus and the Educational Reformation of the Sixteenth Century* by Peter Graves has been republished by Puritan Publications.

Gouge's ministry at Blackfriars was marked by unrelenting dedication. He preached twice every Lord's Day and delivered a well-attended Wednesday lecture for over three decades, drawing ministers, lawyers, and city dwellers alike. His preparation sermons before communion, his visits to the sick, and his personal catechizing of children and servants bore much fruit, with many testifying to their conversion under his ministry.

Not merely a preacher, Gouge was a builder—both of souls and of the physical church. Through his efforts, Blackfriars secured a proper church, vestry, and burial grounds, which were later expanded to accommodate growing crowds. His steadfast refusal of more lucrative positions demonstrated his commitment, often saying, "The height of my ambition is to go from Blackfriars to heaven."

Gouge's writings, including *The Whole Armour of God* and his monumental commentary on Hebrews, reflect his deep understanding of Scripture. Even in his later years, plagued by asthma and other infirmities, he labored tirelessly to complete his work, leaving a legacy that continues to edify the church.

A Life of Godliness

In family life, Gouge was exemplary. He and his wife raised thirteen children, six of whom lived to adulthood, all well-provided for and grounded in the faith. His household was a model of devotion, with morning and evening prayers and consistent catechizing. His meekness and humility were legendary—never once observed in anger, even under provocation.

Gouge's charity was boundless, supporting poor scholars and maintaining a "sacred stock" for the needy. He lived modestly, content with his inheritance and stipend, pouring his resources into others rather than enriching himself.

Faithful to the End

In his final days, Gouge exemplified a holy resignation to God's will, often saying, "I have nothing to do but to die." Though weakened by pain, he continued to express joy in the freeness of God's grace and the hope of glory. On December 12, 1653, surrounded by his family, he peacefully entered the presence of his Savior.

Gouge's life was a testimony to God's faithfulness and a model for ministers and believers alike. As a laborer who, "was not worn out with rust, but with whetting," his ministry reminds us of Christ's promise: "I will give you pastors according to mine heart, who shall feed you with knowledge and understanding," (Jeremiah 3:15).

His works:

Commentaries
1. **A Commentary on the Whole Epistle to the Hebrews**
    - **Volume 1**: Covers Hebrews 1–5 (408 pages)
    - **Volume 2**: Covers Hebrews 6–10 (388 pages)
    - **Volume 3**: Covers Hebrews 11–13 (404 pages)
    Note: Completed by his son, Thomas Gouge, after his death.
2. **An Exposition on the Whole Fifth Chapter of St. John's Gospel**
    Includes additional notes on: John 3:29–36; Mark 1–2; Luke 3:19–20; James 4:7; Genesis 2:9, 7:23; Exodus 12:8, 11, 14–16; Psalm 30:2; Ephesians 5–6 (388 pages).

Theological Treatises
1. **The Whole Armour of God** (766 pages)
    Together with *Domestical Duties*. Also available in French (*L'Armure Complète de Dieu*).
2. **Of Domestical Duties** (339 pages)
    A series of eight treatises:
    - Duties of husbands, wives, children, parents, servants, and masters.
    - The Scriptural basis for these roles.

3. **God's Three Arrows: Plague, Famine, Sword** (494 pages)
   Based on Ezekiel 6:11, with treatises titled:
   - *A Plaister for the Plague*
   - *Dearth's Death*
   - *The Church's Conquest over the Sword*
4. **A Recovery from Apostacy** (97 pages).
5. **The Sabbath's Sanctification** (46 pages).

Sermons and Practical Works
1. **Mercy's Memorial** (31 pages)
   Sermon preached November 17, 1644, celebrating deliverance from persecution.
2. **The Right Way: A Direction for Obtaining Good Success in a Weighty Enterprise** (43 pages).
   Sermon preached before Parliament on September 12, 1648.
3. **The Saint's Sacrifice: A Commentary on Psalm 116.**
4. **The Progress of Divine Providence.**

Unpublished or Hard-to-Find Works
1. **The Saint's Support**: Sermon preached to Parliament in 1642.
2. **A Short Catechism.**
3. **The Dignity of Chivalry**: Sermon preached to the Artillery Company of London in 1626.

Individually Published Works
1. **A Guide to Go to God**: Explanation of the Lord's Prayer.
2. **Strength Out of Weakness**: A progress report on the Gospel among Native Americans in New England.
3. **Briefe Answers to the Chief Articles of Religion**.

The Providence of God:
Christ's Sovereign Hand in All Things
by C. Matthew McMahon, Ph.D., Th.D.

"The lot is cast into the lap; but the whole disposing thereof is of the LORD," (Proverbs 16:33).

So..., the bible tells us, the lot is cast into the lap, but its every decision is from the Lord...*really*? Is that the way *you* see providence? Providence. It's a word that rolls off the tongue easily enough but often fails to find its way into the depth of our thoughts. The doctrine of providence is one of the most sublime and yet misunderstood aspects of God's interaction with His creation. For some, it's little more than a vague idea of divine oversight—a celestial nudge here or a gentle intervention there (usually based on things people like or want to see happen in their lives). For others, it's a source of intense comfort, a living reminder that nothing in this universe escapes the careful *orchestration* of the Sovereign Lord.

But what is *providence*, really? It is more than *chance*. More than what people call *fate*. Providence is God's purposeful sovereignty, His meticulous governance over all things great and small, from the rising of kingdoms to the falling of a sparrow. As the *1647 Westminster Confession of Faith* so eloquently declares, God "upholds, directs, disposes, and governs all creatures, actions, and things, from the greatest even to the least, by His most wise and holy providence" (WCF 5:1).

The Bible presents us with a God who is intimately involved in His creation, orchestrating the events of history for His glory and the good of His people. When we say, "God is in control," we affirm the truth of providence—a truth seen in the parting of the Red Sea, the feeding of Elijah by ravens, and the worst and most heinous event in all of history: the crucifixion of our Savior Jesus Christ on a Roman cross. Every event, whether seemingly trivial or rigorously significant, unfolds according to the wise counsel of His will (Ephesians 1:11).

Providence, however, is not merely a theological abstraction. It is a reality that *shapes* how we live, think, and worship. (It is tied directly to the Regulative Principle of worship). To embrace providence is to walk with confidence, knowing that the God who formed the stars *also* orders the *steps* of His people. It is to trust that even in the darkest valleys, His hand is at work, weaving a tapestry of grace and glory.

The treatises contained in this work explore the depths of providence from three distinct yet complementary perspectives. Each writer, grounded in Scripture and shaped by the theological rigor of their time, brings a unique lens to this vast and glorious doctrine. Let us consider the contributions of Edward Corbet, William Pemble, and William Gouge, as they guide us through the multifaceted beauty of God's providential care.

Edward Corbet: Providence in the Midst of National Crisis

Edward Corbet's treatise on providence emerges from the crucible of national turmoil and spiritual reflection. Preaching before the House of Commons during a solemn fast in 1642, Corbet's sermon, *God's Providence*, takes 1 Corinthians 1:27 as its foundation: "*But God hath chosen the foolish things of the world to confound the wise; and God hath chosen the weak things of the world to confound the things which are mighty.*"

Corbet's primary objective is to demonstrate how God's providence *overturns* human wisdom and power, often working in ways that defy our expectations. He speaks to a nation at war, urging the Parliament to see God's hand in their struggles and victories. His call is both urgent and pastoral: to trust in the God who raises and humbles nations, who appoints rulers and dethrones tyrants, and who, through *seemingly* weak instruments, accomplishes His divine purposes.

In Corbet's biblical view, providence is not an abstract doctrine but a present reality that speaks to the heart of governance and societal order. He challenges the governing authorities to recognize that their power is not self-derived but granted by the Almighty. His message is a clarion call to humility, repentance, and dependence upon God, a timely word for both his age and ours.

Corbet's treatise reminds us that providence is not limited to individual lives but extends to the grand sweep of history. It is a doctrine that shapes nations, directs leaders, and governs the affairs of men. As such, it compels us to look beyond the chaos of current events to the steady hand of a sovereign God, who works all things for His glory and the ultimate good of His people.

William Pemble: Providence as a Foundation of Faith

William Pemble, though his life was cut short at just thirty-two years, left an *indelible* mark on the Reformed understanding of God's providence. His treatise, *God's Providence Over All Things*, explores the breadth and depth of this doctrine with theological precision and pastoral warmth. Pemble's aim is to show that God's providence is not merely an intellectual exercise but a *cornerstone* of Christian faith and practice.

Drawing heavily from Scripture, Pemble emphasizes the all-encompassing scope of providence. From the movement of celestial bodies to the smallest details of human life, nothing escapes God's sovereign *care*. He invites his readers to meditate on the immensity of God's governance, marveling at the Creator who upholds the universe while attending to the hairs on their heads (Matthew 10:30).

Yet Pemble's work is not content to dwell on the grandeur of providence; it presses us to consider its *implications*. How should we respond to the knowledge that God orders all things? For Pemble, the answer is *trust*. Trust in the God who provides for His creatures, who directs their paths, and who works all things together for the good of those who love Him (Romans 8:28). Pemble urges believers to rest in the assurance that their lives are not subject to blind chance or cruel fate but are securely held in the hands of a loving Father. Through Pemble's lens, providence becomes a source of deep comfort and unshakable hope. It is a doctrine that anchors the soul, enabling believers to face trials with confidence, knowing that their God reigns.

William Gouge: Providence in the Life of the Church and the Home

William Gouge, a pastor and scholar of *remarkable* breadth, brings the doctrine of providence to bear on the everyday lives of believers. His treatise, *The Progress of Divine Providence*, takes us beyond the grand themes of history and theology to explore how God's providence manifests in the ordinary rhythms of life.

Gouge's primary focus is the intersection of providence with practical godliness. He examines how God's governance shapes the church, the family, and the individual believer. With a pastor's heart, he calls his readers to see the hand of God in every blessing and trial, encouraging them to respond with gratitude, obedience, and faith.

One of Gouge's key contributions is his emphasis on the *progressive nature* of providence. He highlights how God's purposes *unfold* over time, often in ways that are *not* immediately apparent. This perspective calls for patience and trust, reminding believers that God's timing is perfect, even when it seems delayed.

Gouge also addresses the pastoral challenges of suffering and uncertainty. He reassures his readers that their trials are not meaningless but are instruments of God's refining work. Every affliction, he argues, is filtered through the loving hands of a sovereign God, who uses it to conform His children to the image of Christ.

Through Gouge's work, providence becomes intensely personal. It is not just a doctrine to be affirmed but a reality to be lived, a truth that transforms how believer's worship, work, and walk with God.

Living Under the Shadow of Providence

The writings of Corbet, Pemble, and Gouge converge on a single, glorious truth: God is sovereign, and His providence reigns over all. Together, they present a tapestry of divine governance that is at once majestic and intimate, transcendent and immanent.

Corbet reminds us that God's providence governs nations and history, humbling the mighty and exalting the lowly. Pemble directs our gaze to the cosmic and personal dimensions of providence, calling us to trust in the God who orders all things. Gouge brings the doctrine home, showing us how providence shapes our daily lives and sanctifies our souls.

To understand providence is to catch a glimpse of the mind of Christ—a mind that is infinitely wise, perfectly just, and boundlessly good. It is to see that behind every storm is a sovereign hand, behind every tear is a divine purpose, and behind every joy is the face of a loving Father, and the power of King Jesus.

As we embark on this journey through the doctrine of providence, may our hearts be stirred to greater awe, deeper trust, and more fervent worship of the God who works all things according to the counsel of His will.

In Christ's grace and mercy,
C. Matthew McMahon, Ph.D., Th.D.
From My study, January, 2025
"...search the Scriptures..." (John 5:39).
www.apuritansmind.com
www.puritanpublications.com
www.gracechapeltn.com
www.reformedsynod.com

TREATISE 1:
God's Providence Over All Things
by Edward Corbet

1 Cor. 1:27, "God hath chosen the foolish things of the world to confound the wise."

If we had no other light but that of nature, and no other writings but the book of the world, we might read about God and see his providence. But to find a Savior, to know a Gospel, to understand the mysteries of salvation,[3] is above the art of human learning. Here, the Spirit of God must be our tutor, and the Holy Scriptures alone can teach and give us such a lesson. For God has hidden those secrets from the scribes and great philosophers of the earth. He has cast away the understanding of the prudent as the apostle speaks[4] and has chosen the foolish things of the world to confound the wise.

My text is of a certain nature that will not easily allow a division. I shall, therefore, insist on three

---

[3] Matt. 16:17, John 3:4, 1 Cor. 2:10, John 5:39, Matt. 11:25.
[4] 1 Cor. 1:19.

propositions, which I conceive naturally arise, and which I hope will give the full sense and scope of the words.

First, the Greek word translated, "hath chosen," indicates God's eternal choice, the council of his will, and his providence by which he rules and governs all things. Therefore, from this Scripture I shall take this for my first proposition: PROPOSITION 1: *God's will has an effectual influence on all creatures.*

Secondly, the phrase translated, "the foolishness of the world," indicates that which in the judgment of worldly men is vain and foolish, and that which by God's power is of great value and virtue. Here I will raise a second proposition: PROPOSITION 2: *Foolish things in the judgment of the world are in great esteem with our wise God.*

Thirdly, "to confound" or "make ashamed" refers to that which is weak and foolish and nothing when regarded by carnal eyes, but that confounds many times the greatest power and wisdom. By the hand of providence this brings ruin and shame on that which worldly men most glory and confide in. From this my third proposition: PROPOSITION 3: *God can effect great and glorious designs by weak and improbable means.*

Every proposition affords a great amount of substance for a series of sermons. I can therefore only point at some general topics to these considered here, and as it were, give you a little map of this great country, taking my propositions in the order which I have mentioned.

Proposition 1

The first proposition is that God's will has an effectual influence on all creatures. The nature and condition of God's will, with those distinctions and difficulties disputed among learned men, are either too high for human understanding to reach or else are piously resolved by learned pens already.[5] I shall only touch on the power and providence of this, so far as may support the quieting of our thoughts in these distracted times and give us patience and comfort in the midst of all afflictions. And to this purpose David assures us that our God is in heaven, and he does whatsoever he will.[6] Paul says that God, "worketh all things according to the counsel of his own will," (Eph. 1:11). Justin Martyr and Saint Augustine both say that God's will is the *cause* of

---

[5] Dr. Twisse, Dr. Amesius, Cameron, Peter du Moulin, *etc*. Psa. 115:10; Eph. 1:11. Tract. *de avers. Arist. dogmatum.* L. 4 de Gen. c. 12. And in *En.* c. 96. *Quisquis diffitetur insanit.* Rom. 9:21; Jer. 18:4.

[6] "But our God is in the heavens: he hath done whatsoever he hath pleased," (Psa. 115:3).

all things. What confusion is there that he cannot order? What wisdom is there that he cannot frustrate? What weakness is there that he cannot enable? Nothing is so high that it is above his command, nothing is so low that it is beneath his providence. If the Potter has power of the same lump to make one vessel to honor and another to dishonor, and to preserve or break in pieces what he has made... and the vessel depends on the earth of which it consists, the water by which it was tempered, the wheel on which it was fashioned, and the fire which baked and hardened it all... then how much more shall God Almighty who gives to every creature matter and form, virtue and activity and beauty, exercise his will upon them? How much more shall he build up and pull down, save and destroy, and dispose them as seems good to him? Nebuchadnezzar (one of the greatest and proudest kings ever) will confess as much. As Dan. 4:32 states, "according to his will he worketh in the army of heaven, and in the inhabitants of the earth, and none can stay his hand or say unto him what dost thou?" The armies of heaven acknowledge God in all their ways, legions of angels who excel in strength, who are as full of power as of glory, and who know no law but their *maker's* pleasure. The inhabitants of the earth, men and devils, have this necessity upon them, to obey the Almighty's will, which may appear more distinctly by considering three particulars.

1. Every Creature depends on God.

Every creature essentially depends upon God; they all stand in need of God's *perpetual* help. The hand which made must support, and the power which raised from nothing must still preserve from nothing. Christ confirms this in John 5:17, "My Father worketh hitherto and I work," and Paul in Heb. 1:3, "He bears up all things with his mighty word." 1. As a pillar and sure foundation upon which they stand. 2. As a fountain from which they derive all their virtue and operations. 3. As a sovereign bond by which the parts of all things hold together and are preserved as water in a vessel from dissolution and running out to nothing. He bears up all things without any labor or difficulty, only by his pleasure, his will, and his breath by which they were first made. The creature cannot stand one moment without God's actual support. All things would turn to confusion without his powerful influence who created all things. For the frame of the world is not like a house which will stand on its own after the carpenter has built it, but receives continual subsistence from the Author, who must be perpetually upholding it or else it will suddenly break and fall in pieces. Upon such grounds learned men affirm that preservation is a continued creation, that everything is as it were newly born, newly produced. And although in themselves permanent, yet in respect to God they are in a perpetual forge and dependance.

And as our nature, so are our actions. We cannot utter one word, think one thought, turn our eye, or move a finger, without the concurrence of his power who gives life and breath and all things. Neither can we of ourselves perform anything which is good, direct a wish, or tread one step towards heaven. As the axe is in the hand of him that wields it, without whose elevation it neither cuts nor sinks into the timber, so are we all in the hand of that Master builder of heaven and earth. We are dead and useless tools without his influence, in whom we live and move and have our being. Heavy bodies cannot sink in the water, nor can fire burn that which is most combustible without God's direction. The watery ocean becomes a dry pavement and the hard rock a springing well at the pleasure of the Almighty. The sun of heaven refreshed as a giant to run his course must stand still until the God of heaven concurs to the motion. As it is more labor and strength to support a burden long in the air than at first to raise it from the earth, so may we learn to deny ourselves, to yield up and resign our souls unto God's disposing providence.

Let the Lord deal with me as seems good to him. For dependency is very humble and respective. It studies contentment and is concerned with compliance. It commands the soul to a holy silence, and in all afflictions keeps our hearts from rising up against the Almighty. It makes us kiss the rod, and with the Christians in the same vein as Tertullian, thank our executioners. For shall we receive good at the hand of God and not evil? It is by his great mercy that we do not fall into eternal flames. And so, he uses the calamities of this world which thwart our hopes and prevent our pride or draw us away from that on earth which would have made us more wicked. Shall the scourges of a loving father drive us to impatience or distrust, or make us curse the day of our birth? A soldier is tried in a conflict, and a mariner shows his skill in a tempest. So, shall a Christian faint or fear in the seas of adversity and in the battles of affliction? The candle shines brightest in the dark and the fire burns hottest when the weather is cold. Nature teaches these inanimate creatures to rejoice as it were in danger and to triumph over oppression. For it is empty chaff which is tossed up and down with the wind, unsound corn, and it is the rotten trees which a storm overthrows. Let us realize that smooth and golden steps lead for the most part to lust and carnal security, making us insensible of God's mercies, less regarding of his judgments, and more conceited of our own greatness. Let us consider that the ways of the wicked prosper. They gallop over the green plains of pleasure and plenty, their houses are peaceable, and the rod of God is not upon them. Shall we *envy* the condition of wicked men? Shall we complain because our kingdom is not of this world? Shall we be angry with our blessings? When we consider the grievance itself, we may seek a change in our condition, for we are flesh and blood and who can say his heart is clear? But yet we must remember the Author of our afflictions, the hand which strikes, and the providence which directs them. We may with our Savior desire the cup of suffering to pass from us, but we must also with our Savior desire not our own will, but God's be done. Murmuring only aggravates our burdens and makes them heavier; it cannot remove them. It may increase our guilt and bring upon us new judgments, it cannot take them off. Like a bird that is entangled in the lime twigs, the more she struggles, the more she endangers herself.

2. God is All-knowing and Omnipresent with his Creatures.

What power of man or angel can cloud the eyes of the Almighty? What darkness hides from his face with whom the night shines as the day? The darkness and light are both alike. A heathen will tell you that God is near you, he is with you, he is within you. A father will tell you God is never far from you. The wise and learned men will tell you that God is more present with you than you are with yourself and give good reasons for what they say. And above all, the Apostle Paul tells you in Heb. 4:13 that, "All things are naked and open unto the eyes of him with whom we have to do." Nothing can escape his knowledge; we are as it were exposed without our clothes, without our skin, in the sight of God. But when we are locked in our chambers, the windows shut, the curtain drawn over our heads, when we are compassed about with stone walls, who then shall see us? Indeed, no man can see us, but he before whose tribunal you must one day stand and give an account for every idle word sees you. The good angels see you and grieve at your sin. The devil sees you and rejoices at your folly. The stones in the wall see you and are ready when God pleases to fall upon you and grind you to powder. But God's power does not rest here. His all-seeing eye is not terminated in words and actions. He searches the reigns. He clearly reads the book of our soul; he hears our thoughts. This house of our body, these walls of flesh cannot exclude the rays of that Omnipotent Majesty. David said in Psalm 94 we are fools if we think otherwise. "He that planted the ear shall not he hear? Or he that formed the eye shall not he see?" (Psa. 94:9). He that made the heart, does he not know the ways and works thereof? But God's eyes are purer yet, and I have not expressed the least part of their brightness, for God understands our thoughts afar off (Psa. 139:2). From all eternity he had existence himself, and he was never without existence. From eternity, he has known all the purposes, the secret motions, the deepest root and ground of all our considerations. But who can measure that which is infinite? Our great God knows, which should make us adore and admire and tremble. He beholds us in our proper and corrupt condition. He discerns much filth and great stains in the fairest soul. He sees our carnal thoughts, our worldly thoughts, our presumptuous thoughts, our suspicious thoughts, our partial thoughts, our curious thoughts, our vain thoughts. He sees our wisest thoughts are foolishness, and our best thoughts are enough to condemn us. But oh, worm that I am, ashes, and nothing, and worse than nothing; why do I endeavor to fathom the depth of God's knowledge, to describe that light which looks further and further and has no end of looking further? Whatever God sees (and he sees whatever has been and whatever is, whatever will be or may be, he sees whatever is to be seen and whatever is not to be seen) he rules and governs and commands and directs to his own glory and man's salvation.

O Christian, whoever you are, having fought a good fight, having been made conscious of your ways and having kept yourself straight, in the midst of a crooked generation, do not hang down your head or remit one ounce of zeal in goodness for the reproaches of men or the unjust censures of all the world. But rather revive and quicken your work in every good cause, inflame your holy life, run joyfully in the race of God's service, raise your sad thoughts with David in the consideration of your own sincerity and innocence and singleness of heart, comfort yourself with the example of Christ who despised the shame for the joy which was set before him, and satisfy your soul with Job's resolution, "behold now my witness is in heaven and my record is on high." When you're considering any sinful act, profane company, or vain pleasure, remember the God of Israel sees you. If sinful lusts or base ends reign in your soul and endanger your spiritual safety, call to mind the presence of the Almighty. This one weapon of divine armory is powerful enough to confound a whole world of temptations and to conquer hell itself. For nothing hinders vice so much as exposure; the greatest number of sins are committed because of a lack of witnesses. How tender were the primitive Christians in this regard, for they would not tell a lie to save their lives as Justin Martyr relates. O merciful Father, how are we degenerated from those pious resolutions! What spirit hardens our hearts and devours the conscience of these later generations which make lying a profession? In David's time the fool said in his heart there is no God, but he did not speak it with his tongue. Our atheism is raised to such a height and boldness that we dare profess it in our words and actions; we dare brag of our uncleanness in contempt, as it were of heaven and in scorn of the Almighty.

3. God governs all things to their ends.

God's providence is as general as his creation, governing all things by the same infinite power by which they were made. This glorious fabric of the world would soon lose its beauty and everything would fall into confusion if the hand of providence did not guide their motions and by a sweet command conduct them to their ends. The waters would overflow the earth, the fire would ascend above its proper sphere. Lions and beasts of strength would quickly devour humanity. The creatures have enough destruction among themselves. Divines and naturalists have spoken so much about the use and order of the actions and fabric of rational creatures, of the virtue of plants and stones, that wonder is more appropriate here than words. Let us consider the whole species of mankind, every child of Adam from the point of creation to the last judgment, and when we have considered let us be astonished and cry out with Paul, "how unsearchable are his judgments and his ways past finding out." There is not a lily that grows in the field, not a drop sinks from the clouds, not a hair falls from our head or sparrow on the ground without the eye of providence. Grass has measure and the sands of the sea are numbered. The Lord guides the stroke of every sword in a battle, and not a bullet flies to any other place than where he has appointed.

Those things which are most free and absolute as the hearts and wills of men follow the influence of divine providence, they do whatever they like. Yet they can do no more and in no other manner than God has decreed. He guides them to his own ends, all the while staying consistent with the nature which he has put in them, such that they voluntarily perform that which he predetermined would certainly come to pass. He causes good actions and permits bad actions; he rules and orders all. Absalom refuses good counsel if God so determines, and Eli's sons shall not obey the voice of their father if the Lord resolves to slay them. The heart of the king is in the hand of God as the rivers of water. The king's heart, who has all things at his command and is of all men most free, and whose wrath is as the roaring of a lion, his heart, his will, his favors, his frown, his power, his purposes, are all controlled by God's providence as the waters are carried in their channels at the pleasure of those who have skill to derive them. We all know that Augustus made the general tax to enrich his own coffers, but God used it, as a means to fulfill the prophesy of Christ's birth at Bethlehem. God is the ultimate reason why things are not, why a wise counsel of prominent physicians cannot cure the wounds of a bleeding kingdom, why peace that is desired between two contrary armies finds no success. It is God who hinders and gives way to every work; nothing is independent of him who depends on nothing.

Indeed, Tycho Brahe and Kepler, two famous mathematicians, attempt to counter this doctrine, attributing much to the influences of the stars and other celestial bodies. But God controls and checks them at his pleasure, and nothing certain can be concluded from any of their supposed conclusions but that all creation works together for the best to them that love the Lord. If we can believe that the thousand years mentioned in Revelation for the binding up of Satan is yet to come, we do not need to cast the great fury and confusion of all the world upon the stars nor wonder at those civil dissentions by which we devour ourselves. For when no other enemy could do us any harm, we work our own destruction. The old serpent is such an enemy to goodness and is now so madly furious because his time is short that he brings together all his wicked instruments which are in the four corners of the world to compass the tents of saints about and to strike at the heart of religion, and to banish, if it were possible, the Church of Christ from off the earth.

And yet thanks be to our gracious God, Satan's power is limited both in terms of time and measure and manner. He can go only to the end of his chain (witness Job's afflictions). He may express his malice, but he cannot affect his will. For wickedness itself is under subjection, and all the strength the devil has rests in God. I am confident that these raging waters which so overflow the banks of Christendom are trials of the godly, punishments of sin, and instruments of divine providence. I do not more believe that the sun is in the heaven than I believe that all the calamities which are fallen upon this land shall turn to the benefit of God's people, and that Antichrist shall concur to his own subversion with the very enemies of truth advancing it. When a more full and entire calling of the Gentiles has been accomplished, and the Jewish nation shall be fully converted, then shall the Church of Christ break through the clouds of affliction, prevail over Antichrist and all the instruments of hell, and flourish more in peace and power and glory than ever it has done since men first inhabited the earth.

The great Architect of heaven and earth has in such a wonderful manner engraved as it were his own glorious face, his power, his wisdom, his goodness upon the whole fabric of the world, and upon every part thereof, that this divine face of God cannot be separated from any creature without the creature's ruin and annihilation. I will conclude my first proposition with David's confession in Psa. 40:5, "O Lord my God thou hast made thy wonderful works so many that none can count in order thy thoughts towards us. I would declare and speak of them, but they are more than I am able to express."

Foolish things of the world are held in great esteem with our wise God. How much the heathens of old held the Jews in contempt for their practice of circumcision, that seal of the covenant in the flesh. And although the Socinians of later times do not openly deride baptism, the sacrament of Christianity, and the new birth, they place it among unnecessary ceremonies and consider it a matter of form and custom than of use and power. And do not many approach the Lord's

Supper with unprepared hearts, looking to feed their bodies rather than their faith? Is not the Holy Scripture, which is the word of grace, the word of life, the power of God unto salvation often valued by the Jews less than the Talmud?

The Gospel is the ministry of reconciliation and the ordinary means of eternal happiness, opening the ears, enlightening the eyes, softening the heart, and sanctifying the whole man. So how is it accounted by many as a dishonorable profession? And how do we loath this heavenly manna? What a foolish unnecessary business we make it, preferring our ease, our profit, our private reading before the bread of life and the public worship and service of the Almighty. Such is the condition of the flesh, corrupt reason, and worldly wisdom that cannot relish matters of greatest weight and highest excellency nor discern the doctrine of faith or the mysteries of salvation. I now offer some reasons for these.

REASON 1. God does not see as man sees.

The Lord beholds the heart. He regards sincerity and faithfulness. He loves a willing mind, a kind word.

But men have base and bastard principles by which they judge and by which they are led. They look upon the garment and outward appearances, when the whole world is nothing to the happiness of the soul, and gold can no more fill the spirit of man then grace can fill his purse. Eliab looked more like a king than David in the eyes of Samuel, yet David was elected and Eliab refused (1 Sam. 16:6-7). And that which is highly esteemed among men is abomination in the sight of God (Luke 16:15). How many owe their religion more to education than to the Scripture? How many great books are full of the appearance of truth and yet void of the same?

  I believe if we examine the whole catalog of martyrs and take an exact view of those good souls who put on the whole armor of God and have wrestled with the rulers of darkness and spiritual wickedness, we find the unlearned tradesmen professing Christ and even entertaining death when the scribe and disputer have renounced their faith. How many of Christ's apostles were fishermen, learned only in goodness and better read in sincerity than books? What can be more plain than that of Paul who said, "not many wise men after the flesh, not many mighty, not many noble are called." And this is because the great and studied scholar blessing himself for his deep learning, stands on his own strength and excellency. On the other hand, the illiterate countryman abhors himself, and with all humility and fear casts himself down at the Almighty's feet. Paul goes further and tells us that the wisdom of the flesh is death; it is enmity against God. It is neither, nor can it be, subject to the Law of God (Rom. 8:7). And yet we know that many of God's dearest children have been and still are able scholars, as glorious lights, eminent in every outward excellency as any in the world. Whoever was more eloquent than Isaiah, more profound than Paul? More renowned for all learning than Moses and Solomon? Wisdom and knowledge are happy instruments of salvation when they are guided by truth.

REASON 2: Foolish things are made wise by God's effectual calling.

When God calls any man effectually, he puts his fear into his heart. And Solomon assures us that the fear of the Lord is the beginning of wisdom. When we delight in the commandments of God and devote ourselves to obedience, when we are eminent in good works and abundant in service and embrace religion, then we are wiser than our adversaries, our teachers, and our elders. For wisdom is the fruit of devotion, and because David was holier, he was wiser than his enemies. Piety raises the soul of man and purges it from those lusts which lay waste our knowledge. It inspires the understanding with a high and heavenly light by which we discern the subtleties of the devil, the corruption of our own hearts, and the mystery of salvation. It breathes into our actions *sincerity* and *watchfulness* and the life of *wisdom*. Even if we understand the depths and secrets of life, excel in judgment and sharpness of wit and memory and in a variety of experience and observations, if we do not have Christ, we are blind and stupid fools in terms of any true knowledge. The extent and spirit of all our wisdom is nothing more than learned folly and beautiful simplicity. For tell me, mighty man of knowledge, can your learning resist the devil? Or find out the wiles and devices of the old serpent who is well read in all the arts and advantages of the earth and is as full of knowledge as of malice? Can your worldly wisdom preserve your life one moment longer than God decrees? Can it conduct you to heaven or preserve your soul from hell? That precious soul which St. Basil calls the delight of the Almighty and

St. Augustine the miracle of miracles, that divine, spiritual, eternal soul, when we have continued as many years as there are drops in the ocean, we have not continued one moment in comparison to eternity. After all the ages which men or angels can number or conceive, eternity is only beginning, and is nothing but beginning. And now let the eye of reason judge between a child of God and a man of the world, between the providence of heaven and the wisdom of the flesh, in order to discern what learning it is to know all the secrets of nature and to be aware of the mysteries of grace. What policy is it to have a clear sight into all the kingdoms of the earth and to be stark blind in the kingdom of heaven? What profit is it to gain the whole world and to lose our eternal souls? All the admirable knowledge and virtues of the heathen are but glorious abominations in the God's eyes. And Nicodemus, one of the Pharisees, a ruler of the Jews and a professed learned man in the Law of God is yet stupid and childish in the principles of Christianity. When our Savior talked to him of being born again, he asked if that somehow meant he would return to his mother's womb? The natural man, even when that man is endowed with all the excellencies of which the soul is naturally capable, cannot perceive the things of the spirit of God. For he has neither wisdom to make a right choice of the best end, nor understanding to find out the true means. No, he esteems them foolishness, and so changes the greatest blessing into a fearful curse. Paul gives us the reason, which is because they are spiritually discerned, they require single eyes and soft hearts and humble thoughts; they require a sanctifying spirit. The wisdom of heaven proceeds only from the God of heaven, and therefore,

1. Do not condemn your weak brother.

God can raise his thoughts and direct him to a happy end. He can make him an instrument of glory who is now a subject of weakness and can strike a straight stroke with a crooked stick. Let us remember that we ourselves in times past were unwise, disobedient, deceived, serving lusts and various pleasures. In this way we are clay of the same lump, branches of the same root, and the same grace which supports one may raise another. For who made us to differ? Or what do we have that we have not received? Although the Jews are fallen from their initial standing, yet God is able to graft them in again and to let the day of his glory shine forth upon them. God will remember his covenant with Abraham and Jacob, for his calling is without change. No sin can frustrate *his election*. Those who are enemies to the commonwealth of Israel, and are darkness itself, may be enlightened by the sun of righteousness. God may have children among Turks and pagans; the wilderness may nourish sheep. The thief on the cross became a saint, and persecuting Saul was changed into Paul an Apostle. Other men's imperfections therefore may be our instructions. They may be arguments of great devotion, but they must not be objects of any derision. The least sin deserves contempt, but the greatest sinner charity. Let us hate the vice but help the man, pity him, pray for him. Let us extend our hearts of compassion, wherever there is hope of conversion. But above all let us not despise our zealous brother, who out of a pious apprehension of the joys of heaven and of the torments of hell, of the love of Christ and wickedness of sin, makes much of the least transgression, startles at all appearance of evil, is strict and tender and fearful in all his conversation.

Ignatius the Martyr was of the same mind. "I would to God that I might enjoy those beasts which are prepared to eat me up, I will make much of them, and treat them with all kindness, that they may devour me presently. Let the gallows, the fury of wild beasts, the rack, the tearing and disjointing of all the body, the torments of the devil come upon me, so that I may gain Christ Jesus. For it is better to die for Christ, than to be Emperor of the whole world.

Do not therefore call devotion weakness, or zeal folly. Do not rank them in the calendar of fools who prefer salvation before the world, and by a bold assertion of the truth, fight for martyrdom. God is never more honored than when the kingdom of heaven suffers such violence. The Church never showed more wisdom than when her zeal flamed highest.

Salvation ought to be the business of our whole life. We cannot be more studious to preserve our souls than the devil is to destroy them, we cannot be too careful about that work in which our greatest care is not enough.

2. Do not undervalue God's Ordinances.

Divine Institution sets a price and holy regard to every work: the time, the place, the matter, the manner, every circumstance receives weight from God's command. And he who is not careful to observe the least, does not obey God when he performs the greatest.

For Naaman to be cleansed, he had to wash seven times in the water of Jordan. Washing six times would not remove the leprosy. *God's order* must be observed. It is no excuse to prefer some before others when all ought to be done. It is not the duty of a servant to choose his work or to dispute his master's will rather than obey it. Let the Ordinances of heaven be never so disregarded. They are worthy of precious account, of honorable esteem, of careful observance, in respect to their author and those sacred ends for which they were employed. Common bread becomes the food of life in the sacrament of the Lord's Supper and common water in baptism portrays the remission of sins. The very same words of man which pass as wind and only beat the air, backed by God's authority and blessing shall melt a heart of flint. For his words shall prosper in the work for which they were sent. They are sharper than any two-edged sword.

A scholar will not judge a book by the size of the outside but by the contents. A soldier will not choose a sword by the luster of the hilt but by the sharpness of the blade. Can we then expect God to endure disobedience at the hands of sinful men? Is he less jealous of his honor than the creature? Shall he bring salvation to our doors, to our bosoms while we despise it? Take heed, for curses attend contempt. Famine follows a disregard and unthankfulness for times of plenty. Our Savior called John and James, and without tarrying they left their ship and their father and followed him. We must do likewise, for we are not our own, and therefore we must not set up our own wills, nor judge by our own reason, nor work for our own ends. Rather, we must *sacrifice* ourselves to God, our wills to his will, our reason to his knowledge, the whole of our endeavors to his glory. It is enough for us that he would have it so. His will is wisdom, and justice, and power, and reason, and all things.

3. God can produce glorious designs by weak and improbable means.

What cannot the God of heaven do, in order to set forth his own glory and to advance his servants' good? When all Egypt and any ground upon which an Egyptian breathed was swarming with flies, the Land of Goshen, a little spot of earth in the middle of the country was completely absent of these same flies which, of all creatures are hardest to enclose. Neither walls nor rivers nor armies can oppose their motion or deny them entrance. And yet these active irrational creatures did not enter Goshen when they were round about it. They knew the people of God and made a distinction between his friends and his enemies. Read Joel 2 and you will find a full description of this army of locusts that the Lord sent to punish his people. "Before whom the land was as a garden of Eden, and behind whom a desolate wilderness," (v. 3). "They shall come as the noise of a flame of fire, and devour men like stubble," (v. 5). "They shall march like strong men and go forward in their way without resistance," (v. 7). "They shall fall upon the sword and not be wounded," (v. 8). "The earth shall tremble before them and the heavens shake," (v. 10). And yet this powerful terrible army consists of locusts. What more contrary to good than evil? Or what more opposes happiness more than sin? Yet the evil of Joseph's brethren God disposed to good, and from the greatest sin that ever was committed – that of crucifying the Lord of life – the divine counsel produced the greatest blessing. Bitter waters shall be made sweet by salt, and the sacrifice shall burn when water is poured on it. In the same way, our afflictions are mastered and ruled by

God's injunction on them to further our salvation. Our wounds are remedies, and those who contradict the precepts of the Almighty are, actually obeying his Providence.

1. God uses means but does not need them.

The Lord of Hosts can conquer without an army, "Neither by power nor might, but by his spirit," (Zech. 4:6), he can subdue every mountain of opposition and bring about whatever he has determined. Indeed, in the ordinary course of Providence, second causes do concur to bring about a worthy virtue. Yet here also the God of Providence has the governing power; he is the Author of all the good which is produced and may be said to work himself though with other means. For all the world of creatures are but instruments which, at their best, contribute no assistance to Almighty God but rather depend on him for their being. They work by his continual influence and receive their ends from his eternal order. The same reasons which moved God to make the creatures, move him still to use them, not out of necessity or lack of power but from love and goodness. Did he not cast out devils with his finger (Luke 1), and can he not beat down men with his hand? Did he not make the world when there was no help, and can he not rule the world without any help? Is his arm shortened who is omnipotent? Or his providence decayed who is wisdom itself? God is not like the children of men who can do nothing without their tools. He can work above means, and he can work against means. And sometimes he disables the greatest means, and sometimes he uses no means at all.

2. God can help the means.

He that can work without means can improve and advance the weakest means and dispose little occasions to great purposes. Luther, an obscure friar, shook the whole kingdom of hell, and through him God gave truth a resurrection and a conquest over heresy. Naaman was healed by the common waters of the Jordan; the blind man cured by clay and spittle. Empty pitchers struck more fear into the army of Jericho than a hundred cannons. The Moabites thought they saw the blood of their enemies when they saw nothing but the sun shining in the water. And yet this was their overthrow (2 Kings 3:22). God shows strength out of weakness and pulls down the pride of the flesh to a shadow.

1. Therefore, do not trust in *means*.

The way to have something taken from us and not blessed is to trust in it and depend too much on it. "Thus saith the LORD; Cursed be the man that trusteth in man, and maketh flesh his arm, and whose heart departeth from the LORD," (Jer. 17:5). For when we make flesh our support and strength and rely on it for deliverance, our hearts withdraw from the living God and we deify the creature. The Lord himself speaks as much in his discourse with Gideon in Judges 7, "The people which are with thee are too many for me to give the Midianites into their hands lest Israel make their vaunt against me and say my hand hath saved me." Self-sufficiency and creature-confidence emanates from a vaunting and rebellious spirit. It sets up itself and dethrones the Almighty. "Woe to them that go down into Egypt for help, and trust in chariots because they are many, and in horses because they are strong," (Isa. 31:1). And if you wonder what this woe is, the prophet tells you in verse 3, "When the Lord shall stretch out his hand, the helper shall fall, and he that is helping shall fall, and they shall all together fail." Curses and woes follow them which rest in and lean on earthly things, and the fruit of carnal confidence is destruction. How many parents lose their children by setting their hearts too much on them? Let us therefore exalt the power of the Almighty, *adore his Providence*, trust in his goodness. Let every Christian endeavor to join his soul close with God, to bring his trust only to the God of trust and to set him in his own place, the highest in the heart. For the conjunction of the soul with God is the life thereof, and while we are careful to preserve that union, the gates of hell cannot prevail against us; we stand impregnable. But if the devil can come between God and our souls, and if the love of the creature and confidence therein make the least separation and unloose our hearts from their highest good, then our rock and sure footing is gone. We lie open to that roaring lion and to those waters of iniquity which will quickly sink us in perdition. Despair, idolatry, atheism, and the whole body of sin have free passage into our souls. Every degree of departing from God is distrust and unbelief, and what sins will not an unbelieving heart commit?

2. *Serve* God's providence in the use of means.

So far as God affords us helps and means, we must not be found lacking in our duty to actuate their power and to employ them to the best advantage. We must go along with providence, and serve occasion and opportunities, and be exactly careful of all means while not trusting in any. God promised Joshua not to leave him nor forsake him, yet he bids him be strong and of good courage. The Israelites must fight it out even though God had given the enemy into their hands. Indeed, sometimes he will have us only be spectators of his actions, he will tell Jehoshaphat and the people of Judah to, "stand still and behold the salvation of the Lord", when he is pleased to show a strange deliverance and to get honor in the confusion of his enemies as he did with Pharaoh in the Red Sea (Exod. 15:4). In such cases there is no second cause; he will fight himself to do his own work with his own hands. But most commonly he requires the service of the creatures which he does not need and sets down a course of means which he will not alter; and then it concerns us to *answer providence with industry*, to put forth our strength, and to use such means as God offers. If we have the honor to be God's instruments, then we must faithfully perform the office of instruments and be active. We must cast our care on God for the issue, all the while sweating ourselves in the prosecution. Hell itself shall never prevail against the flock of Christ. And yet they must strive to enter in at the narrow gate. They must work out their own salvation with fear and trembling. Election to the end includes the means, and whoever will be happy in another world must first be good in this. Presumption is as dangerous as distrust, and he may justly lose the fruit of a happy end who neglects the use of lawful means.

3. Confide in God in the absence of means.

It was a pious speech of Luther in a letter to Melancthon, "God is able to preserve his own cause from falling, or to raise it when it is fallen. God is never more near his people than when deliverance seems furthest off." This war which we think will devour us all may be as much an instrument of preservation as the whale which swallowed up Jonah was a means to bring him to the shore. The depths of mercy are beyond the depths of misery, and God has his own ways of helping his children when everything else denies them help. Moab and Ammon, the enemies of Judah, destroy one another. God is mighty in power and excellent in working, for though our sins are many and our transgressions are great, yet God's mercies are more, and his glory will be greater in pardoning. No faults can dam up the endless goodness of the Almighty; we cannot offend so much as he can pardon. The enemies may be many and mighty and cruel, yet Ahab with a few young men vanquished Benhadad's great army and 32 kings with him. Remember that repentance preserved Nineveh which in 40 days was to be destroyed (Jonah 3:6-10) and faith delivered Daniel out of the lion's mouth (Dan. 6:12-28). He who will raise our bodies can mend our worst condition. Was Abraham deceived, who trusted in God for a son against the course of nature? Or the three Hebrew children who believed God would deliver them out of the fiery furnace? "O Lord my God in thee have I put my trust, save me from all that persecute me and deliver me," (Psa. 7:1). He will deliver us if we pray to him. And pray to him we will if we *trust* in him. For *trust* is the root and life of successful prayer. Let us all therefore pray and trust, trust and pray. And after our prayers let us trust again, that seeing it is all one with the Lord, to save with many or with few, to help with means or without means. Let us pray therefore, and trust continually, and let us never cease to trust and pray.

AMEN

Sermon Authorization.

It is this day ordered by the House of Commons that Master Corbet shall have thanks returned him from this House for the great pains he took in the sermon he preached this day in the city of Westminster, at the request of this House. And it is ordered that no man shall presume to print his sermon but he himself, whom the said Master Corbet shall authorize in his own handwriting. And it is further ordered that Sir John Corbett, a Member of this House, shall return the thanks to Master Corbet.

TREATISE 2:
The Providence of God
By William Pemble

To the Reader:

To the gentle reader, all welfare and happiness:

See, learned reader, you have here an excellent and wonderful discourse of that great scholar in which both the light and law of divine providence is plainly set before you fully and expounded. A treatise most worth reading, for I think this does much avail us to know the providence of God itself, though we do not know the manner and reason of all acts which usually are incident to the view and consideration of divine government. Of this at least we ought to be most assuredly persuaded, that God our Father is over the whole world and above all other things, and does sweetly and wisely look to man's actions, not in general only, but even in *particulars*. Nothing can be done by us without the divine power, nor ought to be done without a holy acknowledging of that power. Indeed, the knowledge of that high providence is so necessary to all Christians. For what strengthens our faith more, or reforms our life, than the knowledge and acknowledgement of God's providence? It is evident that whichever way the godly turn their eyes, the devil has innumerable hindrances of piety ready, especially in these last and worst times. But when we are once firmly settled upon this belief that God who is all-seeing cares for all things as if they were but one, and for all particular things as if he had but one thing to care for, easily afterward are all the evil's snares discovered. Courageously we will still run forward in the course of godliness. For out of this doctrine, easily and abundantly enough, will we gather all those things which are needful to implant faith in us aright, and rightly to order our conversation.

Almighty God, who holds all things in his hand, I pray that this discourse concerning providence may happily serve both for the benefit of the church and the increase of piety. *Amen.*

Thine in Jesus Christ,
RICHARD CAPEL

The Providence of God

The works of God are:

1. Personal, which are done by a single principle; namely of the persons, according to their proper and personal relation. And these are:

A. Simply personal[7], whose term of beginning and ending is regular. Such are the works of relation, as to beget, to breathe, *etc.*

B. In some respect[8], whose term of ending is common, namely, the creature.

And the common principle of action is in the three persons. But the proper term is in one only as:

-Creation of the Father.

-Redemption of the Son.

-Sanctification of the Holy Ghost.

Essential, which come from a common principle, namely, the essence, and are terminated in the creature. As the outward works, which are done by all the persons, meantime keeping the distinction of order.

These are either:

Inward, in counsel or decree, or outward in execution. Of them both in general.

---
[7] These works belong not to the will working by deliberation; but to nature, working necessarily.
[8] These are voluntary.

Concerning the end of theology and the divisions of God's works. The chief end of theology in respect to man is life or salvation eternal whereof there are two degrees: 1) More imperfect and begun in this life, namely, exceeding joy and peace of conscience, first, by assurance of remission of sins and of punishments due, together with reconciliation. Secondly, by the beginning of sanctification and of our conformity with God, with a hope and taste of future perfection in both. 2) The other more perfect and finished after this life, arising out of the full fruition of God when body and soul will be perfectly united[9] unto God, and by that union the soul will be conformed to God in understanding and will and the body made incorruptible and glorious; both of them remaining exceedingly glorious in the highest heavens[10].

As to the matter of our salvation, it is considered in two ways. 1) In its causes, which are God's works and effects, and 2) In its subject, namely, man and his lost estate.

Not only has God decreed good things from the beginning of creation, but also (in justice) the evil works of evil men that the glory of God in his justice and mercy may be manifested through it, as 1 Peter 3:17 states, "If the will of God be so." And this decree is the acting principle of all things and the cause of all causes. For God decrees what he wills, and what

---
[9] John 14:3 and 1 Cor. 15:28.
[10] John 14:2-3, Peter 1:4, and Phil. 1:21

he wills he does effectually. And yet though it is a necessary principle, it does not take away either the liberty of the will toward a thing or the nature and property of a second cause, but orders and disposes to the end appointed. The effects may be contingent or necessary, as was the nature of the second cause (compare Acts 17:3 with Matt. 25:39). Christ died necessarily, and this work or act of God is internal, forever abiding within his own essence itself.

2. The execution of the decree is an act of God, whereby God does effectually work in time all things as they were foreknown and decreed and works that they exist and be actually. Of this there are two parts:

1. Operation, or effectual producing of good things which are, and which come to pass.

2. Operative permission, whereby God first permits the same work to be done by others out of a voluntary permission as noted in Rom 1:26, "God gave them up," and Rom 9:15, he is free to give his grace to whom he will. Secondly, he works efficiently,[11] as this is the nature of God. As Gen. 13:20 states, "God intended it for good," and likewise Gen. 45:7 and Isaiah 10:15. 1. As it is the punishment of sin: but punishment is a moral good, because it is a work of justice. 2. As it is a mere act or action, and 3. As it is a chastisement, exercise of faith, martyrdom, or satisfaction for sins as was the death of Christ.

---

[11] By governing and ordering.

This action of God is external, a temporal act passing from God to the creatures. But just as the decree is of various kinds, so also the execution of it.

1. There is a common and general decree in terms of all the creatures, and includes:

-The decree of creation

-The decree of government or providence.

2. There is a special decree which belongs to reasonable creatures, angels and men.

It is called the *decree of predestination*. And it consists of the decree of election to save and reprobation to damn some angels and men.

1. Execution of the decree is common in regard to both the decree of creation, which is creation, and execution of the decree of government and preservation, which is providence (the works of nature).

2. Execution of the decree is special in regard to the decree of election of good angels and their confirmation in their estate and elect men through their redemption, restoring, and all the gracious works of God.

And execution of the decree of reprobation of evil angels by their thrusting down from their estate and punishment in hell and men and their rejection, hardening, punishments, and all effects of divine wrath.

This therefore will be the order of what is to be said, that first, we speak of the executions of the more common decrees. Because of the decrees themselves, we have only a little, either laid down in Scripture or doubted among men. Next, we will address the special decree, and its execution by the various decrees of it. The first chapter will be of creation, the second of providence, the third of predestination and in the fourth (by the assistance of God's grace) we will address redemption and the several parts of it, that is, its means and subject.

Of Creation

Inherent in the work of creation is a twofold manner of our knowing it. The first is common knowledge, namely as the whole nature of things and in the time of creation which flowed from that common principle. And special, according to the proper nature of everything in his kind and every single thing. This branch of study belongs to natural philosophy but is also proper for theological consideration.

Creation is the action of God whereby out of nothing he brought forth nature and all things in nature and completed them in the space of six days. He did this to his own glory and salvation of the elect. To consider the nature of it more fully, four things must be considered.

1. The efficient cause, which is God. The moving cause, the Father; the working cause, the Son; and the perfecting cause, the Holy Ghost (Acts 17:14, Col. 1:16, Heb. 1:1-2, Gen. 1:2,

Ps. 33:6, Job 26:23). The world, or universal nature of things, was not from eternity, but began when the creator saw fit to begin it according to his will and counsel. Everything that was made was made by him. And these things persuade us to believe assuredly. Principally, through faith (Heb. 11:3) which is grounded in the holy Scripture (as in Gen. 1 where we have the history of the creation), and Job 37, 38, and 39, Psalm 104 and 136, almost the whole of Isaiah 40 and 21, Psalm 33:9, Job 9:8, Rev 4:11, Rom 11:36, and Isaiah 45:12. Secondarily we have the light of nature shining forth in these reasons.

First, the origins of nations laid down by Moses (Gen. 10 and elsewhere) which could not have been pretended by him.

Secondly, the beginning of arts, the first inventors and the age every one of them flourished is manifest. And it is not probable that for so many ages before this mankind lived without the arts, and that they were all invented and perfected in these last times.

Thirdly, the recency of all heathen histories, the most ancient of which don't tell of anything before Noah's flood or the beginning of the Assyrian empire under Ninus, and the sacred history itself is only around 4,000 years. But it would be a shameful reproach and disgrace for those men who lived so many ages before, if we should say they were either so slothful or ignorant that they would not or could not deliver in writing the things done in their times.

Fourthly, the certain order of times from the beginning of the world to the appearing of the Messiah.

Fifthly, the decay of man's body and age, which from a greater strength and time of life is now dwindled down a good many years. But if it had always been so decaying in those presumed infinite ages prior, by this time it would have been brought to almost nothing.

Sixthly, the certain order of causes and the impossibility that they should go on in perpetuity. There was need for some first or universal cause. But this does not occur apart from God. For in so many kinds of mixed bodies, which by continual succession are generated, there must needs be a commonality or singularity of kind which was either eternally beforehand and afterward ceased to be, or began in time and was produced, though not by some natural cause for there was none but supernatural, namely, the omnipotence of God. But if it be said that all mixed bodies were indeed created in time, produced and framed out of simplicity, and those that are simple, out of a first matter coeternal with God, we must earnestly deny that there can be any eternal substance which is not God. For then there would have to be two first things, which is impossible. Besides, whereas all other things are imperfect, it is needful that they borrow their being from something that is most perfect.

Seventhly, the testimony of all sound antiquity, which being taken from the very voice of nature and sense of truth, ought to be esteemed of some weight in this business. For the consent and universal authority of all, especially the[12] wiser sort, has assigned to the world an origin and beginning.

Eighthly, as a thing is, so it works. But God in his essence does not depend on another. Therefore, neither does he require previous matter in his working.

Ninthly, art presupposes nature, and nature, matter. But God, who is a more excellent cause, presupposes nothing.

Tenthly, the first cause (namely, God) is infinite and therefore can do whatever is non-contradictory. But the creation of things in the beginning of time does not imply a contradiction.

Therefore, by these reasons it is evident that the world is not eternal but rather was created in time by the great Workman of all things. It could not exist from eternity if God did not create it from eternity. Though creation can be known by the light of nature, if we consider only the light of nature, no reason can be presented which plainly demonstrates the process of creation. Some say the world could have been created from eternity. Yet when questioning whether something could be brought forth by God from eternity, they affirm that not only spiritual substances, as angels, but bodily forms also that are subject to corruption (as men and other

---

[12] Philosophers, poets, and Aristotle himself who seems our greatest adversary. *Rhe.* 2.23. *de gener.* 2.20. sect.58.

creatures) could have been made by God from eternity and also could have been preserved to an infinite space of time. And they dare also to affirm that this is not in contradiction to either God creating, or the things created, or the very nature of creation.

It may suffice to know that the world was created of God in the beginning (Gen. 1:2), that is, in the beginning of time, or together with time, rather than in time. For the first instant and moment of creation was the beginning of all time that followed, and not the end of any that went before.

2. The matter of creation is two ways distinguished, as creation itself is twofold: primary and immediate. And of this creation there was no matter at all as ancient as God or existing by him. For God gave nature a beginning immediately by himself. And whereas God is of infinite power, by his divine power he brought forth the nature of things, not out of some previous matter but out of *mere nothingness* and that which did not exist. *And in this way were created,*

1. All spiritual, immaterial, and super celestial substances, as the angels, the highest of heaven, and the reasonable soul. For those things which are void of matter cannot be framed out of matter.

2. This first principle is of all corporal and material substances and that subject out of which they were all made and do consist. Namely, the first matter, that huge lump, a rough and indigested heap, dark and obscure, partly of water,

partly of earth, as it is described by these conditions (Gen. 1:2). Moses called this matter "earth;" others call it "the chaos." This matter is void of all second form, distinct and specific. Formed, namely, with a common[13] first form, but afterward, by the power of God, to have put on the special forms of all simple bodies and mixed.

First, it seems no probable reason can be given for creating this confused chaos, out of which afterward all things should come forth distinct. It was easy for God, and certainly much more glorious, to first create the kinds of all things distinct and perfect, then afterward to frame them of matter created beforehand except when there is an evident reason for the divine counsel, as in making man.

Secondly, it is against nature that the first matter should subsist, separate and by itself, under some common and general form. We cannot conceive how this should be done nor whether God (who is not the author of confusion) would approve of it being done.

Thirdly, this matter did not exist without form, as these do interpret, but under the specific and distinct forms of two natural bodies, earth and water, as is described in very clear words in Gen. 1:2. But some common form could make no distinction. Neither can the first matter of all things be called either earthly or watery.

---

[13] Kock. Fyst d. log. 1.I. Sect.2. cop.17.

Therefore, by those words, "In the beginning God made heaven and earth," we understand a general proposition which is to be explained afterward in particulars.

And in this way the primary and immediate creation now follows the other, secondary and immediate, when a thing is brought forth of matter that was and existed before, yet so rough and undisposed that it may be esteemed as nothing. So man was created of the dust of the earth (Gen. 2:7), and beasts and birds out of earth (verse 19). This God did merely of his good pleasure, no necessity urging him, and no power inherent in the matter he used helping him.

3. The form of creation may be considered, either in respect to God, or in respect to the things created.

In respect to God it is this; that God created the world, not by necessity of nature, but according to the eternal and unchangeable decree of his own will, that by his word alone, without any change, weariness, endeavor, or labor, he made all things and established them. And he did all freely and easily.

In respect to the things created, the form is either,

1. Internal: namely, the very force and power of nature was fashioned by God, both on all things in a common manner and fashion and also on the several kinds, according to the particular essence of everything, and its conditions, by which they are enabled unto their proper or common operations.[14] Or,

---

[14] All creatures were made according to external shapes in the mind of God, Acts 15:8, Exodus 25, to the end. Now these shapes in God differ not really

2. External: Creation occurred in a moment with respect to singular bodies considered apart. Yet with respect to them all, it was not perfected in an instant but rather in the space of six days. The differences of days do not note a succession of the same action in time, but the order of various divine works that declare both the power of God in bringing out what effects he would, even without natural causes, affording light to the world, making the earth fruitful, and bringing trees out of it even before the sun and moon were created. Further, this declares his goodness and liberality by providing for the creatures which were not yet made and bringing living creatures into the earth.

In order that we should consider the works of creation diligently and distinctly, let us look at the works of each day by themselves.

The work of the first was fourfold. First, that of heaven which is understood under various names as, 1) highest, first, and unmoving heaven. In Scripture it is called the[15] heaven of heavens (Acts 1:11, Eph. 4:10, 2 Chron. 6:18, Psalm 148:4). 2) The heavenly angels: the knowledge of whom is either more

---

from his essence, but are themselves the essence of God conceived by him, as it is by the creatures unchangeable. And these shapes are eternal and immutable. Which in working God necessarily looks to, and follows without varying. An artificer may as occasion serves, change his intended plot. God not so, for in God all things that can be done are contained and do shine forth. See Polamus *Syntag.* 5.6.7.

[15] Also the third heaven paradise, sanctuary, country, Abraham's bosom. This heaven is corporal, though subtle and shining.

common or more particular in terms of the estate of angels (either of their integrity or fall), as well as their offices and ministrations. These we will treat partly in the next chapter concerning the providence of God (whose ministers the angels are), and partly hereafter, when we consider sin. 3). In regard to heaven, we may also consider the heavenly spheres, likely also created on the first day. In other words, they were likely made the first day, but without the lights of the stars means they were not beautified until the fourth day.

The second and third works were the earth and water joined together. "For the water did overflow the earth and compassed the whole face of it."[16]

The fourth work was light, which is altogether extraordinary because it is not manifest in what subject it remained. Was it in the surface of the water or was it in the fire (which doesn't yet seem to have been made on the first day), or the spheres of heaven, which is more likely?[17]

The work of the second day was 1) the firmament, that most vast space between earth and heaven including the elements of air and fire. This space is called heaven in verse 8 and in very many other places of Scripture. 2) The division of the upper waters from the lower, that is, of the clouds which

---

[16] Which mass was called empty and void, in respect of that most beautiful ornament which was afterward to be brought into it.
[17] Yes, altogether the truth.

are in the middle region of the air, from fountains, rivers, and the sea, which are under the lowest region.

The work of the third day was threefold, 1) the gathering of the lower waters into one place which was called sea, 2) the drying of the earth that it might be fit to nourish plants and living creatures, and 3) the bringing out of herbs and plants of all sorts (Gen. 9:13).

That of the fourth day was the lights, both greater (sun and moon) and lesser (the other stars).

That of the fifth day, fishes and birds, and of the sixth day, a twofold work, 1) all living creatures that were earthly, and 2) man, being male and female. God made Adam of the dust of the earth so that in his bosom he might ever carry the evidence of humility so as not to produce pride against God because of his excellency. And he made Eve from a rib of Adam, to be a sign of how close they were and of the love to be held between man and wife. But with man the creation ceased. Not only was man the most perfect piece of God's workmanship, he was also the end to which all the rest were ordained. For the rest of the creatures, by the creator's bounty, were subjected as servants to Adam as their prince and master.

Out of all these things which have been spoken of creation arises the goodness of the creature, which is the excellence of natures put into it by the effectual working of it. Void of all defect, deformity, or evil, both of fault and punishment. For all things that were made were very good (Gen. 1:13).

Again, goodness is twofold:

1. General in regard to all creatures, namely, the entirety and perfection of all gifts and natural powers, whereby the creature could exercise his operations in conformity to God's will, orderly, to the right end.

2. Special in terms of the reasonable creatures (angels and men) who were beautified with supernatural gifts, called holiness, or the "image of God," (Gen. 1:26). This we will speak to afterward when we deal with the threefold estate of man.

So, of the form of creation, in the last place remains the last and chief end of the workman, which is the glory of God the Creator in manifesting his power, goodness, and wisdom. These eminencies of God, shining forth in the existence of all creatures, their excellency, order, and wonderful[18] workmanship, God would want to be acknowledged and praised by reasonable creatures (Psa. 19:1, Prov. 16:4, Psa. 104:24). But the nearest end is for the work itself, that all things by their several uses may serve man, especially to the furthering of the salvation of the elect (Gen. 1:28; Psa. 8, 4:56; 1 Cor. 3:22).

After creation follows the doctrine of God's providence. For as things could not have been without God, so neither can they continue without his providence. The next thing therefore

---

[18] Also, the most wise government and administration of things, as Isaiah 40:26.

is that (as much as we can) we explain the administration of God in governing and preserving the world. Wherein two things come to be seen: 1) that there is providence, whereby the world is governed and what it is, and 2) that it is denied by many because in many points it is obscure and difficult.

To the first, that there is providence which governs the world (though many deny it wholly, believing God neglects the care of particular things and only moderates and governs the actions of universal causes). Yet the church believes and teaches that nothing is done in the world without the certain and determinate counsel of God, and the truth of this most certain and most necessary foundation of all religion fences itself with strong arguments against all errors and odd opinions.

We look at his providence first from the works of God which demonstrate a most wise order of things. From both a natural and a civil perspective, these works could not have originated from blind nature, or chance, or fortune. Secondly, we will reflect on providence from the laws of nature. Thirdly, from the perspective of peace or torment of conscience, according as the law has been either kept or broken. Fourthly, from the perspective of punishments and rewards in accordance with men's deeds, which prove there is some judge of the world and revenger of wickedness, whose severity we cannot shun. Fifthly, from the perspective of heroic motions, virtues, and singular gifts given by God to princes, magistrates, inventors of arts, artificers, and others for the common benefit of mankind. Such helpful instruments he also takes away when he is about to punish a nation or generation. (There are a very many examples found in every age of the world.) Lastly, from the perspective that reasons there is a God, proves there is both God and providence.

Taken from the causes (namely, the attributes and nature of God):

1. There is a God and therefore providence.
2. The omnipotent will of God, whereby all things are done without which nothing can come to pass.
3. His infinite wisdom, whereby he can be present with all things done in his kingdom, so that nothing is without his direct oversight.
4. His justice in distributing rewards, and punishments, and goodness, whereby he communicates himself to the creatures.
5. His foreknowledge of all things, unchangeably dependent on the counsel and decree of God.
6. He determines the ends of things, therefore also the means to those ends.
7. He is the first cause, therefore on him depends the second. And nature, as the instrument of God, being acted upon by that universal principle, works. And then being stirred according to itself, works other things.

Now we see what providence is. By providence we do not mean foreknowledge or fore-ordering of all things in God, but the temporal and external *execution* of this decree in the actual administration of things. So that providence is an external and temporal action of God whereby he preserves, governs, and disposes all things as well as singular things (both the creatures and the faculties and actions of the creatures) and directs them both to the mediate ends, as well as to the last end of all, after a set and determinate manner, according to the most free decree and counsel of his own will, that he himself in all things may be glorified (definition of providence).

In opening this definition, we must include three things,

1. The object of providence.
2. The degrees of providence.
3. The kinds of providence.

1. For the object of God's providence, or the matter about which it is concerned, is (in a word) all things which 1) are and have a permanent nature. Whether they are the substances and essences of creatures, spiritual or corporal, considered in what manner so ever, both generally and specially, commonly and particularly in the singular things, and 2) accidents, as the quantities and qualities of all things, and not those only which belong to common nature, in its original and entirety, but also those which are of a particular nature by some failing and defection. And both of these kinds are subject

to God's providence, as in respect to nature, so also in respect to use, as they are initially ends (last or intermediate), or secondly, means to those ends, whether ordinary or extraordinary, necessary or contingent.

These objects have a flowing nature which includes all the actions, operations, and motions of the creatures, as well as their passions that are either natural (without any act of the will – an example would be his appetite which is led by the instinct of his natural will: as to live, eat, drink, *etc.*) or voluntary, which proceed from the will which is reasonable and intelligent, as of angels and men. This is known as man's elective will.

As to the qualities of man's actions, they are either good or bad. To all these things, not only those which are great and excellent, but also the smallest and vilest, the providence of God extends itself. This truth is affirmed in various Scripture passages (Eph. 1:5; Psalm 94:8; Acts 17:25, 28; Eccl. 3:1; 1 Sam. 2:3; Lam.3:37). Also see Matt. 6:26 and 30, Job 37:2 and 38, Isaiah 51:15, and Psalm 135, by which the care of God for all living creatures, all meteors, and the like is described. Also concerning voluntary things and actions of men, good and bad, as shown in Prov. 26:1 and 9, Jer. 10:23; Psalm 139:1, 33:13 and 15:15, and Job 12:20. Concerning honors (Psalm 75:6-7), calamities, diseases, punishments, and the like (Amos 3:6; Job 5:18, 12:14-15; 1 Sam. 2:6-8, and Isaiah 45:7). The ends of common wealth (Dan. 2:21, 4:32 and 35), concerning the actions of particular men as Cyrus (Isaiah 45:13), of all kings (Prov. 21:1), of the Jews against Christ (Acts 4:27-28), of the king of Assyria, (Isaiah 10:5), of Joseph's brethren (Gen. 45:8, 50:20). Also concerning things that are contingent (Exod. 21:13), as the slaying of a man unaware (Prov. 16:33), as well as in the calamities of Job (Job 1:21) and the fall of sparrows (Matt. 10:29-30).

Providence therefore is as largely extended as the universal being of things. Nothing escapes the insight of God, not even the very trifling matters of things. But he also guides them and orders them according to the pleasure of his will. Not a sparrow falls to the ground, nor a hair from our head, nor a leaf from the tree, without the providence of our heavenly Father. As they have being by the power of God, creating and preserving them, so also by the wisdom, providence, and goodness of God they are disposed and determined to their end. They are because God would have them be. Neither would he have made small things if he despised small things. In this way we have the object of providence.

Next follows the degrees, or parts, or various gifts of God's providence as they are exercised on the objects above referenced. These are, 1) preservation: providence according to dispensation, which is twofold. First of existence, which is the continuing of things created, both mankind and creatures and the rest which God (by continued succession and generation) makes to be perpetual. And singular things, which are preserved by God for a while, so long as he pleases. Secondly, of virtue, which is the upholding and moving of the proper abilities of every creature which belong to the actions and perfections of it. Both are described in Acts 17:28, "In him we live, and move, and have our being," and 1 Tim. 4:10 where he is called the "Savior of all men."

The act of governing, by which God as a monarch, orders and disposes of all things and governs them according to the freedom of his own will. This government is altogether monarchial, and most orderly; for it is one, supreme, most absolute; and the authority is God's power. It is an absolute and entire dominion, and right in all the creatures, that he may determine of them whatsoever he pleases and dispose them to ends as he thinks good. The action of God in governing, is in general twofold:

1. Permitting, or providence by permission. This is when God does not restrain the actions of the creature but permits the will of the agent, and when he allows that which he could immediately hinder, as he allowed Adam to fall. Another example is when he allowed the Jewish nation, his chosen people, to go after other idols, hardening their hearts.

2. Accomplishing and working: providence according to his good pleasure. This is where God performs whatever is good in nature, common or singular. This is seen and discerned *many ways:*

First, in setting down laws. This is when God as supreme monarch and lawgiver provides reasonable creatures with the laws and rules of working. Secondly, in executing justice, or distributing rewards and punishments when God defends and rewards his good subjects and punishes rebels. Thirdly, in ordering. This is when God disposes all things, and all their actions and motions to his own order (though they are very confused) and to their certain ends, and also brings them there by his admirable wisdom. In this ordering, God does three things:

First, he appoints to all things their own ends, either proper and immediate which are natural, or that common, last, and supernatural end, which is his own glory, in his justice and grace. Secondly, he disposes all means toward these ends. Thirdly, being so disposed, he promotes them effectually. And by ways known to his divine wisdom, either revealed or secret, he brings them to the ends appointed.

We also speak of them more particularly in relation to singular subjects, or objects of providence. *Therefore*,

1. The natures and essences of things, and all the accidents of entire nature, are subject to God's providence – all those ways of preservation, government, efficacy, and ordering. But the accidents of nature, when it is hurt and failing, are governed by permission and ordered effectively.

2. The ends of things, and means of whatever sort leading to those ends, are in every way appointed, governed, and ordered by that most high providence.

3. All actions, natural and voluntary, are subject to God's providence. First, preserving, for God preserves the nature of things as well as the liberty of the will. Secondly, governing effectually and moving them. For that, God as a universal principle moves all others that they may work. Thirdly, ordering, for that God disposes and brings all actions of the creatures to the ends appointed for them.

4. Concerning necessary and contingent things, God's decree is unchangeable. For that which God has decreed necessarily comes to pass, yet most freely, because he could from eternity either not decree it, or decree it after another manner. In this way the world was necessarily made, and in this manner too (see Matt. 26:53-54).

Secondly, of second natural causes, which are so made by God that they cannot work other than they do, but are limited to one of the contraries, which yet might either not be at all, or be hindered, or changed by God. Therefore, fire burns necessarily, yet by God the fire at Babylon was hindered from burning.

Thirdly, of being, either of the cause, or the thing caused. For a cause which might have wrought contingently and contrarily, yet when it works one way, cannot choose but work so. In like manner, that which was contingent whether it should be or not, yet when it was, or is, it cannot but be, or have been because two contradicting things cannot both be true.

Contingency is unchangeable, opposite to necessity, and it is twofold:

1) In general: namely, the manner and nature of things requires that some be necessary and some contingent. First, there is the liberty of God's will, or of the will of angels and men. Secondly, the changeable and unsuitable nature of elementary matter, and the fitness and inclination of it unto various motions.

2) In particular: in respect to all particular causes and effects, between which there is a changeable and uncertain dependence. And that occurs in a threefold regard and respect:

First, in terms of the power and liberty of the first agent and first cause, which alone being unchangeable in his nature, at his pleasure can change all the powers and operations of second causes that either they may not work or may work after another manner than they would by nature. For although they are ordained of God to certain effects, yet they are changeable and subject to divine providence which works by them. And therefore nothing in the world is so certain but God can make it uncertain, except for those things which would necessitate contradiction.

Secondly, of their own proper nature, which God has put in second causes. When of their own natures they work contingently and are not limited to one effect more than to another but are indifferent and equally disposed as the blowing of the wind, the motion of living creatures, and the actions of man's will.

Thirdly, of some accident: when by the working of a cause that moves by itself there follows contingently (by something that falls out) an effect to which the cause was never ordained, either by its intention or nature – as it happens in all accidental causes, or voluntary, wherein there is fortune, or natural in which there is chance. For example, when a man shoots an arrow and kills a crow that flies by unaware, or when a shellfish which the eagle drops out of her beak to break it, breaks on top of the poet's head who sat upon the rock instead. These examples, and hundreds like them, show the connection and order which is between the seeming cause and effect which is altogether contingent and changeable if you respect the proper nature of that cause.

For these reasons we may likely hold that it is an effect and work of God's providence that a thing comes to pass, whether contingently or necessarily. If it comes to pass necessarily, it is because God ordered that it should come to pass necessarily, and therefore contingently, because he would have it be contingently. For God has put this nature and properties into things, and according to the manner of things appointed and continued by himself, so works (either mediately or immediately, as a universal principle) that things are disposed both ways – of necessary causes come necessary effects, and of contingent, contingent effects.

2. It is one thing to come to pass necessarily, another contingently, another infallibly. These two note an order between the cause and the effect, but in as much as both contingent things and necessary things come to pass infallibly, but those contingently, these necessarily. Therefore, note here two profitable rules:

The first is that all effects are determined to be either necessary or contingent, not from the first and remote cause, but from the nature of immediate causes, being either necessary or contingent.

The second is that necessity of consequence doesn't take away contingency, and therefore all effects, which may rightly be called necessary, or rather infallible, in respect to the prime and universal cause, namely the decree and providence of God. And yet in respect to the second and nearest cause are worthily counted contingent. Wherefore providence doesn't take away the liberty of man's will, which it in no way enforces.

Thirdly, out of all it appears that God's providence is conversant about things contingent and necessary 1) by preserving the natures and beings of them both, 2) by governing them efficaciously or permissively, and 3) by disposing them to the appointed end.

And in the last place we must dispute good and evil actions: how the efficacy of divine providence is knowledgeable about them. Of those that are good, there is no controversy, for these he wills simply. All the difficulty is about evil actions. We will consider this briefly.

There is a twofold evil:

1. Of punishment, as all destruction, affliction, or desertion of the reasonable creature by which God punishes sins. The evil, though to the creature it is evil, in itself is a moral good because it is an execution of the law and declaration of justice. Wherefore God, the judge of the world, and one that shows his justice and glory, wills it, does it, determines and ordains it (Jer. 28:8; Amos 3:6; Isaiah 45:7).

2. Of fault, which has a double consideration of both good and evil. For although there is a chief good which is God, yet there is not a chief evil, which is not joined with some good. For chief evil takes away all goodness, both natural, and moral; and so, it wholly destroys the subject and at last turns into mere nothing.

Now *sin is*,

1. Evil in and by itself, as it is a defect and deformity, contrary to the nature, justice, and goodness of God. And God does not will simply, nor works, nor approves, nor furthers sin. Psalm 5:4, "Thou art not a God that wills iniquity." God's permission, in terms of the very formality of sin is a mere suspension of will and denying of all efficacy about sin. Because, so far as it is sin, and in that it is sin, God neither wills nor produces it, inasmuch as the will, which is infinitely good,

neither wills nor produces anything but what is very good. It is said that evil, as evil, might not have been if God had not allowed it to be. We say it is one thing to will the nature of evil, another to will the existence of it. For in that the will is terminated in the very evilness of evil, or in evil as it is in itself evil, which cannot be affirmed concerning the will of God without blasphemy. But in this it goes further and is terminated in the existence of evil. And this is a good thing, for it is good that evil *is* or exists. But to will that evil have being is not to will the evil in itself, but for the event.

God preserves what he has given, and by his power he determines their motions, freely inclining them to any indeterminate actions. And he upholds the will as a thing of nature by a common principle and moves natural and voluntary actions by a singular principle.

In many places of Scripture there is evidence of concurrence of God about evil actions, as in Gen. 45:8, "It was not you that sent me hither, but God." And in Deut. 2:30, God hardened the spirit of Sihon. Psalm 105:25 states, "He turned the minds of the Egyptians, that they hated his people." God, in and with the evil works of men, performs his own good work. Now this concurrence is not a bare and idle looking on, but a working permission; it so permits that in the meantime it does something efficaciously and positively, and that in three ways.

1. By withdrawing grace and help when the creature is forsaken in working and left to itself. As in Adam, God denied

him effectual counsel, by which the strength of his will, which he had sufficiently, might effectually resist sin.

In this also he withdraws light, by not enlightening the mind with the acknowledgement of his will, as in Deut. 29:4, "God gave them not a heart to understand," not revealing his will to the creature, by which he would have the work accomplished (Rom. 14:22-23). When help is withdrawn, the creature sins necessarily indeed and yet freely. It cannot choose but to fall and err; yet inclines to that fall and error of its own accord and by its own fault, not by enforcement and compulsion of God's will. For as the sun causes darkness not by infecting the air but by hiding its light, and a staff falls to the ground not thrown by the hand but forsaken; and a country, destitute of inhabitants, abounds with wild beasts, not by the man's fault, but for lack of them. So, God is the author of sins not by infusing malice and some vicious quality into the hearts of men, or by bowing their wills inwardly and efficaciously, or compelling them to evil, but by forsaking them in their action and by not bowing them to obedience, that they may be conformable unto God (because of their own accord they tend to ruin and sinfulness). We seduce and corrupt ourselves when left to ourselves. By him we stand, but of ourselves we fall and perish by our own fault. For when he that permits has power to hinder, though he is not bound to do so, and he to whom permission is given has power to work, yet without compulsion, on both sides the act is voluntary, in the former without any fault and in the latter without excuse.

2. God as a common principle preserves and stirs up nature and the actions and motions which are according to nature, the motions and inclinations to sin being stirred up first by removing those impediments which were a hindrance to sinning freely.

3. By limiting sin. While he prescribes a means to the actions of sinners, he also limits their ability to sin, so they are allowed to do no more harm, either to others or the sinner himself, than God thinks fit (Psalm 76:10 and Prov. 16:9).

Secondly, in terms of the end, sin is good. Because by reduction it tends to good. For God by his admirable wisdom draws good out of it and orders it unto that which is good. Sin in itself is disorder and confusion. Yet through the infinite wisdom of God, it is disposed in very good order, and regardless of its own nature and will of the sinner, is turned and brought to good. A prime example is the great sin of the Jews in crucifying the Lord. If our judgment on this plan were consulted, there would be confusion at every turn. But the hand and counsel of God predetermined all these things, and by a most wise order disposed them to an end far most excellent. For with God in charge, behind everything that happens there is a very good order of justice and goodness (1 Cor. 14:33). And sometimes it is also manifest.

God therefore *wills sin*, in light of the end of it and to what he orders it, *which is,*

1. The manifestation of his justice in the righteous punishment of the sinner, whereof the highest degree is to punish sin with sin. This is why God willed the hardening of Pharaoh's heart (Exod. 7:3-4), and of Sihon's heart (Deut. 2:30), the cursing of Shimei (2 Sam. 16:10-11), and the lying of Ahab's prophets (1 Kings 22:23). He deceived the people by false prophets and the false prophets themselves (Ezek. 14:9) and all enemies of the truth (2 Thess. 2:11). "Thus he gave up the Gentiles to their own lusts," (Rom. 1:24, 28). "He sent the Jews the spirit of slumber, eyes that they should not see," *etc.* (Rom. 11:8). In these and like places, God as a most just Judge[19] punishes some former sins with the latter and makes way for the deserved punishments of both.

2. Correction and trial, so by false prophets God tries his people (Deut. 13:3), by heresies he proves those who are good (1 Cor. 11:19), and by sins takes down the over confidence of his own, their pride, and other evil affections.

3. Declaration of mercy[20] in freeing us from the corruption of sin by the help of grace and freeing us from guilt and punishment by the merits of his son's blood (Rom. 5:20-21).

---

[19] So, the judges at Athens gave condemned malefactors poisonous hemlock to drink for punishment of their misdeeds.
[20] Thus he gives an antidote against the force of poison.

4. In all these God sets forth *his own* glory.

In the last place, there remains to discuss the kinds of it, which may best be comprehended in a threefold distinction.

1. Providence is divided into mediate and immediate. Mediate is when God governs creatures by creatures, as by means and instruments. For God uses the ministry of second causes, both natural and voluntary, either men or angels, which are the most excellent instruments of providence in governing the world. Evidence of this appears multiple times in Scripture, in which their ministry is set forth; both generally in Heb. 1:4, "being made so much better than the angels, as he hath by inheritance obtained a more excellent name than they." And verse 14, "Are they not all ministering spirits," *etc.*, Psalm 103:20, "Bless the Lord, ye his angels, that excel in strength, ye that do his commandments," *etc.*, and verse 21, "Bless the Lord, all ye his host: ye ministers of his," and Psalm 104:4, "Who makes his angels spirits: his ministers a flaming fire," and specially above the good and elect, Psalm 91:11, "For he shall give his angels charge over thee," *etc.*, and about the wicked, Psalm 35:5, "Let them be as chaff before the winds and let the angel of the Lord," *etc.*, as well as Isaiah 37:36, "Then the angel of the Lord went forth," *etc.*

Of this mediate providence, three things are to be noted. First, God uses means not for lack of power in himself but of his own free will, in the abundance of his goodness. Secondly, providence includes means, which if we neglect (unless God has revealed that he will not use them) we tempt him without being aware of it. He that ordains to the end ordains to the means. Thirdly, God also uses evil instruments beside and beyond their own intention: as the Jews and Joseph's brethren.

Immediate providence is when God by himself, without the ministry of the creatures, preserves and governs things. So, he governs immediately and preserves the first and universal causes of things. In this way the apostles were called (Gal. 1:1).

2. Providence is identified as general, by which God takes care of all things which he made, Psalm 36, "Thou, O Lord, save both man and beast," and special, by which among the creatures, he looks to men especially. And among men, especially to his elect, with a fatherly care, as 1 Tim. 4:10 confirms.

3. Providence is also categorized as ordinary, when God governs the world, and things of the world, according to the order and laws which he himself set in creation, and extraordinary, when he works either against or beside that order so appointed, as in the working miracles.

FINIS

TREATISE 3:
The Progress of Divine Providence
by William Gouge[21]

Preface:

To the Right Honorable House of Peers Assembled in Parliament

Right Honorable,

As in various other ages and places, so in this age and place where we now live has my text been verified, and that within the compass of these last five years. In every one of these years, God has done better to us than at our beginnings. We have great and just cause to hope that he will yet continue to do better and better.

It was a special evidence of God's good providence that the great counsel of England was called at the time it was called. The State of Church and Commonwealth were so far out of order that without a Parliament it would not nor could not (in man's apprehensions) have been redressed.

---

[21] September 24, 1645.

The Reformation that was then intended by that Parliament occasioned an Act to prevent inconveniencies, which may occur by the untimely adjourning or dissolving of this present Parliament. What better thing could have happened to this State? The good consequences that have occurred as a result are evident demonstrations of God's mind and will to do better and better for us.

When might the good providence of God have been better discerned in protecting the person, upholding the spirits, directing the counsels, and prospering the endeavors of such as were assembled in a Parliament than in this? When might the same providence of God have been better discerned in stirring up men's minds, encouraging their spirits, enabling their bodies, and preserving their persons for maintaining a cause than in this cause that is now maintained by the Parliament? Of them who with a single eye behold the footsteps of the Lord in the counsels of our Parliament, it may justly be said, "They have seen thy goings, O God, the goings of my God, my King," (Psalm 68:24). Have not our armies had success beyond expectation, and even to admiration? What good progress has been made in Reformation? And may we not yet hope that God will do better to us than at our beginning? God's promise is the ground of hope: and my text shows that God has promised as much.

So go on, Right Honorable, and put forth your utmost endeavors, for bringing on those better things that yet remain. Where there is hope, endeavors should be most earnest; for hope stirs up men's spirits to set upon great things.

Though the full accomplishments of the remaining better things should be reserved to a future age, yet it becomes us to be as earnest in prosecuting them, according to the ability and opportunity that God gives us, as if we ourselves were sure, while we live, to have their fruition. For experience shows it to be true which of old was said of the husbandman, that he plants trees which may be useful in another age. But I hope that God will let you sow and enjoy the fruit of your counsels and of our desires. This shall be the continual prayer of-

Your Honor's humble servant and orator,
WILLIAM GOUGE

Ezekiel 36:11, I will, *"do better unto you than at your beginnings."*

Among other evidences of God's special providence[22] and care over his Church, this most special one that he ever afforded it is the sufficient means to instruct it in his will and direct it in the way to happiness.

When at the beginning he made man, he did not only write his law in his heart. He also revealed means of standing in his happy estate or falling from the same. For example, consider the two sacraments in paradise: the tree of life, and the tree of knowledge of good and evil.

When men increased into a family, God ordained the firstborn to be both a governor and an instructor of the family.[23]

When the church multiplied into a nation, God set apart the twelfth part, namely one tribe of twelve, to be ordinary ministers therein. These he distinguished into Priests and Levites.

---

[22] God's care in affording instructors to his Church.
[23] Sundry kinds of instructors 1. God himself (Genesis 2:9) 2. Firstborn (Genesis 4:7, 18-19). 3. Priests and Levites (Numbers 3:12).

When that age ended, he ordained pastors and teachers to be ordinary ministers in his Church,[24] to the end of the world.

Of old in extraordinary times and upon extraordinary occasions, God imbued men with an extraordinary spirit. These men were described as prophets.[25] Such a prophet is Ezekiel of whom, I suppose, more extraordinary visions and revelations were made known than to any other. He was raised up in one of the most corrupt and sad times, even when God was forced "to do his work, his strange work, and to bring to pass his act, his strange act."

He prophesied in Babylon,[26] where he was carried captive when the Babylonians first entered into Jerusalem and took away many of the sacred and precious vessels of the temple, together with a large portion of the treasures of that house and of the kings and princes, and carried them, together with Jehoiakim the king and many of the princes, priests, and people into Babylon. There he also continued after the Babylonians had again entered Jerusalem, broke down its walls, and burned the house of God and all the houses

---

[24] 4. Pastors and teachers (Ephesians 4:11).
[25] Extraordinary prophets (page 2.)
[26] When and where Ezekiel prophesied (Isaiah 28:21 – page 2).

in the city, carrying away the remainder of the vessels of the temple and its treasures, together with Zedekiah and the king, and the remainder of the princes, priests, and people.

About the same time Jeremiah was raised up to be a prophet among the remnant of Judah which was left in Judea. They both prophesied the same things in terms of substance, though they were far distant in place, and so ratified each other's prophecies.[27]

As other prophets, so this our prophet had to do with two sorts of people – wicked and pious. The wicked were either openly profane and impenitently obstinate or covertly hypocritical and deceitful. The pious were righteous, upright and humble. In which respect his prophecies were of a mixed kind. In regard to the former sort, he had such a spirit as was given to Boanerges, sons of thunder, to denounce God's terrible judgments against them.[28] And in regard to the latter, he had such a spirit as was given to Barnabas, a son of consolation, to pronounce sweet promises (Acts 4:36).

---

[27] *Jeremiah & Ezekiel immimente capri vitate vaticinium exercuerunt: sed alter earum in terra suda alter in Babylonia. Hier com. In Jer. Prophet. 1.1* With what kinds of persons prophets had to do.
[28] Different spirits of prophets (Mark 3:17).

By this the obstinate were the more terrified and kept down; the humble and penitent were supported.

The spirit of consolation sweetly breathed forth in this chapter out of which I have taken my text. It is full of very comforting promises.

In the beginning, he points at the insults of enemies against the Church of God in their troubles, by which weak spirits are often perplexed. Therefore, to keep their spirits from fainting, by his prophet the Lord makes known beforehand the good which he intended for them. Many particular promises are set down, both before and after my text, but the sum of them all is couched in these words translated, "I will do better unto you than at your beginnings."[29]

The Hebrew is so excellent in compounding words, as it comprises the ten words of my text in two, which mean, word for word, "I will do good above your beginnings."

The first word encompasses under it all the blessings which God intended for his Church. And not of the Jews only, but of the Gentiles also, from the point of their return out of captivity until the coming of Christ. And not in the flesh only, but in glory also. The

---

[29] The sum of the chapter.

latter word relates to all former ages of the Church, even to those very times of their great troubles.

The main scope of it all is to set out *the progress of Divine Providence.* [30]

This is done by five particulars.[31]

First, the author or fountain. He is not expressed in the text, though clearly intimated. For the verb is of the first person, which is associated with the particle, "and" intends the same person that is mentioned before. Thus, "I will multiply, I will settle, and will do," that is "I will do." In the seventh verse the person intended is plainly expressed as the Lord God. And in the next clause after my text, the Lord Jehovah is expressed. For where this word LORD is set down in four capital letters, it indicates Jehovah.

Secondly, the act by which the aforesaid providence is exercised, "do good." The word is in the third active conjugation of the Hebrew tongue, called "Hiphil," which signifies *efficiency.*

Thirdly, the increase of that providence is indicated as "above" or "more than." Our English comprises the act and the increase thereof under this

---

[30] The scope of the text.
[31] The parts thereof.

word "better," for better sets out "more good," or "greater good."

Fourthly, the parties to whom that good is intended, "unto you." I must confess that the parties are not expressed in the original though implied under this copulative particle "and" which shows that this promise is made to the same parties to whom the former were made; and they are thus expressed, "I will multiply upon you," and "I will settle you," so here "I will do better unto you." They are, in a word, "Israel," under which is comprised the Church of God.

And fifthly, the times are the latter times; for this promise is made in opposition to former times, expressed under this word "beginnings."

These five points afford five useful instructions.

First, *the Lord is the fountain of all good.*[32] I may well say all, for the indefinite particle "good" intends as much. Besides, all the particular good things promised before and after my text are applied to its author the LORD, as are other good things also in other places. And so, the apostle states, "Every good gift, and every perfect gift is from above, and cometh down from the Father of lights," (James 1:17).

---

[32] Observation 1. (page 5).

Secondly, *God causes his goodness to flow forth.*[33] He is not only a full fountain, but an open and overflowing fountain (Zechariah 12:1). David speaking to the Lord of his goodness, thus says, "Thou art good, and do good," (Psalm 119:68).

Thirdly, *God's goodness ever increases.*[34] It is like the waters that came down from the Lord's Sanctuary and increased from ankle deep to knee deep, from knee deep to mid deep, from mid deep to an impassable river (Ezekiel 37:18). In this respect, this word of comparison, "better," is used to note the good things which God provides in latter ages. I intend to exemplify this in various particulars hereafter.

Fourthly, *the Church is the proper object of God's goodness.*[35] Israel, to whom this promise was explicitly made, broadly includes the Church of God (Malachi 1:2-3). This is further evidenced by that great difference made between Jacob and Esau, thus expressed, "As it is written, Jacob have I loved, but Esau have I hated," (Romans 9:13). The apostle applies this to God's chosen children on the one side, and all the other on the other

---

[33] Observation 2.
[34] Observation 3.
[35] Observation 4.

side. Therefore, there is a special affirmation of God's mercy in relation to the members of the Church; for he is said to be the Savior of all men, especially of those that believe (1 Timothy 4:10).

And fifthly, *the best things are reserved for the last times.*[36] The beginnings here mentioned (comprising all former ages and times), in addition to the great increase of goodness here intended, must by default refer to the latter times. Therefore the prophet expressed, "It shall come to pass in the last days, that the mountain of the Lord's house shall be established in the top of the mountains, and shall be exalted above the hills, *etc.*," (Isaiah 2:2).

Time will not allow me distinctly and fully to handle all these points, neither indeed is it needful. For the last comprises all the others under it. So it is that we can express it as, "The Lord has provided his better things for the latter times of his Church." Here we have:

1. The person that is the fountain of goodness expressed, *the Lord.*
2. The act of goodness flowing from him, in this word, *provided.*

---

[36] Observation 5.

3. The comparison, better things, declares the *increase* of his *goodness*.
4. The mention of his Church shows the proper object, or parties to *whom* his goodness is extended.
5. The times are here expressly set down, in these words, *latter times*.

Therefore, in handling this doctrine, "God has provided his better things for the latter times of his Church," all the former will be proofs for this; the former will prove all the rest. My purpose therefore is to insist upon the last doctrine. You heard it before, hear it again, "God has provided his better things for the latter times of his Church."

Let us observe the particular good things which God has provided for the Christian Church, which is the Church of the latter times, and you shall find them to indeed be better.[37]

The testament given to the Christian Church is a better testament (Hebrews 7:21),[38] made by the Son of God, Immanuel, God with us, and ratified by his death,

---

[37] Particular things described as *better*.
[38] 1. Better testament.

wherein an eternal inheritance is bequeathed to us (Hebrews 9:15). Was there ever such a testament before?

The covenant made between God and his Church in these latter times is a better covenant (Hebrews 8:6). Allow me, because mention is made here of both of a testament and a covenant, to show you the difference between them.

1. A covenant is an agreement between two: a testament is the *declaration* of the will of one.[39]

2. The two between whom a covenant passes must be both living: a testament receives power by the death of him that made it (Hebrews 9:17).

3. A covenant is ratified by the mutual consent of both parties: a testament by the will only of him that made it.

4. A covenant includes conditions for both parts: a testament depends on the mere favor and grace of the testator.

Now the covenant made with Christians is better than the former two covenants, both called old, because they are both in many respects nullified.[40]

---

[39] Difference between *covenant* and *testament*.
[40] Two old covenants.

1. The first was a covenant of works made with man in his entire estate, which by his fall he made impossible for man to keep.

2. There was a covenant of grace made with the Church before Christ was born. However, this covenant contained such obscure promises and prophesies, and dark types and shadows, that in time it was needful for it to be abolished. But the new covenant made with the Christian Church is so clear and revealed that it may well also be called *better*.

3. The promises now made are better promises (Hebrews 8:6).[41] Most of the promises before Christ's incarnation were of temporal good things, though I will not deny that spiritual and celestial good things were prefigured under them. But now spiritual and heavenly good things are more expressly, clearly, and plentifully promised to the Church.

4. The hope that now we have is a better hope (Hebrews 7:19),[42] as promises are the ground of hope. The better the promises, the better the hope must needs be. And in those respects the promises are also better. Christians may more immediately, directly, and steadily

---

[41] 3. Better promises.
[42] 4. Better hope.

hope for all spiritual and heavenly blessings than they that lived before Christ could.

5. The sacrifice that we now have is better than the former sacrifice (Hebrews 9:23).[43] He that considers the difference between the bodies of unreasonable creatures and the body of Christ the Son of God cannot but know that there is an infinite excellency in this sacrifice over and above those. If anything under the gospel may justly be called better than its counterpart under the law, surely this sacrifice may most of all be better than those.

6. The blood of Christ, in regard of the cry of it, is better (Hebrews 12:24).[44] It is said "to speak better things than that of Abel," because Abel's blood cried for vengeance. Christ's blood cried for pardon. Christ, when he was on the cross where he shed his blood, cried, "Father, forgive them," (Luke 23:34). Also, Christ's blood is better than that blood which was shed on the altars under the law: "For it is not possible that the blood of bulls and goats should take away sins," (Hebrews 10:4) but the "blood of Jesus Christ cleanses us from all sin," (1 John 1:7).

---

[43] 5. Better sacrifice.
[44] 6. Better blood.

7. To insist upon no more particulars,[45] the apostle comprises all those good things, which in comparison to the Church of the Jews are bestowed on the Christian Church. For this he said, "God has provided some better thing for us, that they without us should not be made perfect," (Hebrews 11:40).

In as much as gospel blessings are called "better," they are also called *new*[46] as, "A new covenant, a new testament, a new Jerusalem, a new heaven and earth, a new name, a new commandment, a new way, a new heart, a new spirit, and a new song." These and other like things are called new, in contrast to old things which decay and vanish away; so there was a necessity of new things to succeed them (Hebrews 8:13).[47] These new things shall never grow old; they are new, not only in their beginning, but also in their perpetual continuance. They shall ever be fresh and flourishing, like Aaron's rod which budded and bloomed blossoms and yielded almonds. And so always continued even as long as the ark of the testimony remained before which it was set (Numbers 17:8 and Hebrews 9:4). The new covenant and the new testament are the same, which were before

---

[45] In the margin *All Gospel things are better*.
[46] Gospel-things new.
[47] In what respect *new*.

termed "better," and in such like respects called new. Of them therefore I shall need to say no more than what has been said. The rest that follows are these.

First, a new Jerusalem.[48] The old Jerusalem was of senseless corruptible materials. The new Jerusalem is of lively stones, a spiritual house (Revelation 3:12, 1 Peter 2:5). It is called the "city of God," because of its excellency (for excellent things, in Canaan's language, are said to be things of God), and because of both the care which God takes of it and the delight which he takes in it. The old Jerusalem was but a type and figure of this.

Secondly, the new heavens and a new earth (Isaiah 65:17):[49] Hereby is meant a new face of a Church far more glorious in its spirituality than the former before Christ. The phrase is hyperbolical: it is used to set forth not only a renovation of the Church, but such a renovation as would put the world as it were into a new form and frame; insomuch as he that attentively looks upon it might say, "Behold new heavens and a new earth." Speaking of the times of the gospel, the apostle says, "We look for a new heaven and a new earth," (2

---

[48] 1. New Jerusalem.
[49] 2. New heavens and a new earth . *Non dixit alios caelos & alia terran videbi muo sed antiquosia melius communtatos.* Jermome. *Com in,* Isaiah 65.

Peter 3:13) ⁵⁰and thereby referring to the glory of the world to come.

Excellent matters are sometimes spoken of in their progress and sometimes in their perfection and consummation. So the new heavens and the new earth, in their beginning and increase may be both under the gospel in time, and in their consummation and perfection after the day of judgment.

Thirdly, a new name (Isaiah 62:2).⁵¹ This Christ calls "his name," (Revelation 3:12.) This name is to a son of God, "for as many as received him, to them he gave power to become sons of God," (John 1:13). Of old, they were called children of Israel; now they are called Christians (Acts 11:26), the name the apostle gave to the mystical body of Christ, consisting of many saints (1 Corinthians 13:12).

Fourthly, a new commandment (John 13:34),⁵² that is, another kind of commandment than that which was written in tablets of stone. For that exacted an impossibility (Romans 8:3) by reason of the weakness and corruption of our flesh. But the new commandment

---

⁵⁰ How we still look for new heavens and a new earth. *Principium in novotionis in praesentiseculos perfecta consummaton novitas nondum.* Jerome. *Com. in* Ephesians 1:2.
⁵¹ 3. A new name.
⁵² 4. A new commandment.

is written in the fleshly tables of our heart, by which ability is given us cheerfully and acceptably to perform the same.

Fifthly, a new way (Hebrews 10:20).[53] This is also called a "living way," which Christ by his flesh has consecrated for us. For Christ himself, having with his own blood entered into the most holy place, has thereby made full satisfaction for all our sins (that which makes the way to heaven impassable), making the way easy for us to walk in. Therefore Christ is, "the way, the truth and the life," (John 14:6), and the only true way that leads us to life.

Sixthly, a new heart (Ezekiel 36:26).[54] This is opposed to a man's natural heart, which is called "a heart of stone," in that it is so obstinate that it will sooner (like a stone) be broken all to pieces and utterly confounded with God's judgments than yield to him and his word. This new heart is not only freed from that obstinacy but is also made flexible and pliable to the word of God and works of his spirit, and thereupon is called "a heart of flesh."

---

[53] 5. A new way.
[54] 6. A new heart.

Seventhly, a new spirit (Ezekiel 11:19).[55] This also is opposed to a man's natural spirit, which in all things resists the good spirit of God. Such a spirit the Jews of old had, of whom Stephen, the fifth martyr for Christ, thus speaks, "Ye do always resist the Holy Ghost. As your fathers did, so do you," (Acts 7:51). But this new spirit readily and willingly yields to every good motion of the spirit of God.

Eighthly, a new song (Isaiah 42:10).[56] A song which shall sound forth, "God's praises from the end of the earth," by reason of the gospel, whose sound as the sound of the heavens, "has gone forth through all the earth," (Romans 10:18). The sum and substance of this new song was sung out by a heavenly choir at the birth of Christ. It was this: "Glory to God in the highest, and on earth peace, good will towards men," (Luke 2:14).

Finally, to insist on no more particulars, there is a promise to make all things new (Revelation 21:5).[57] If any shall think that this is meant of the world to come, let him consider how expressly the apostle applies it to the time of the gospel; saying of that time, "Behold, all things are become new," (2 Corinthians 5:17).

---

[55] 7. A new spirit.
[56] 8. A new song.
[57] All things new.

Therefore we see how this promise of God doing better for his Church in the latter times is evidenced by many different particulars, of better and new things.

Yet further, as if ordinary words and usual comparisons were not sufficient to set forth the great increase of God's providence, the prophets use very transcendent and hyperbolical expressions,[58] in order that we may grasp it according to our capacity. To which purpose this increase of God's providence is thus expressed: "For brass I will bring gold, and for iron I will bring silver, and for wood, brass, and for stones, iron," (Isaiah 60:17). Here he shows that as wood is better than common stones, iron better than wood, brass better than iron, silver better than brass, and gold better than silver, so much better, yea infinitely more, are the good things of these latter times better than the good things of former times. Yet further is this increase heightened, "The light of the moon shall be as the light of the sun and the light of the sun shall be sevenfold, as the light of seven days," (Isaiah 30:26). Who does not understand what a great difference there is between the two lights of the moon and the sun?[59] To make the light of the moon

---

[58] In the margins: *Hyperboles* do set out the increase of God's goodness.
[59] Isaiah 65:1, 18.

as great as that of the sun would indeed be a great increase. And because there can be no greater light than the light of the sun, he multiplies that light to the number of perfection, saying "The light of the sun shall be sevenfold, as the light of seven days." And to show that no comparisons are sufficient to set out the increase of God's goodness to the full, it is further said, "The sun shall be no more thy light by day, neither for brightness shall the moon give light unto thee: But the Lord shall be unto thee an everlasting light, and thy God thy glory," (Isaiah 60:19).

If we take a view of the increase of God's good providence, generation after generation, even from the beginning of the world to the end thereof, it will yet more clearly appear that as God's goodness has ever increased more and more, its greatest increase has been in latter times, and so the better things are reserved for us and others who have lived therein.

For an even clearer example, we will consider the whole continuance of the world[60], together with the world to come, as one great week; and distinguish the whole course from the creation to the day of judgment,

---

[60] The continuance of this world divided into six days.

into six long days, the seventh, being an eternal Sabbath, or rest after the day of judgment.

The six aforementioned days may be distinguished as:

The first from Adam to Noah. Besides God's goodness in creating the world, he also manifested that great evidence of mercy in promising a Redeemer to free man from his miserable bondage under Satan, where he had plunged himself. The words of the promise are these, "It shall bruise thy head, and thou shalt bruise his heel," (Genesis 3:15).

By this relative particle "it," the seed of the woman, the Lord Jesus Christ is being referred to here. The words being spoken to Satan (the serpent) by the head is meant Satan and all his power which, by bruising, denotes an utter subduing of the same. The next words, "Thou shalt bruise his heel," show Satan's attempts against the mystical body of Christ and his troubling of the same in many respects. But take note that it is the heel only and not the head that can be crushed. This was a very gracious promise, and a great good.

The second day lasted from Noah to Abraham (Genesis 6:18). During this day, the Church had the knowledge of God's preservation of it from that common deluge which destroyed the rest of the whole world. The type of Christ here was represented by the ark. This the apostle calls, in relation to baptism, a like figure (1 Peter 3:21). For it set forth to the Church such a preservation and deliverance from sin and destruction as baptism does. In this respect, a more express evidence of God's goodness was given in this day than in the former.

The third day was from Abraham to David, wherein that precious and express promise of blessing all nations in Abraham's seed was made and wherein Israel was also brought out of Egyptian bondage (a type of the redemption of the Church from her spiritual bondage under sin and Satan). In this day the tabernacle, with the many other types of Christ, as well as his offices and benefits to his Church, were first ordained, and Israel settled in the land of Canaan, a type of their heavenly rest. Therefore did this third day far exceed the former in glory.

The fourth day was from David to the carrying of Israel into captivity. In this a royal government was given to God's people (a type of Christ's royal kingdom). Herein most of the extraordinary prophets (special types of Christ's prophetical office) were raised up, and clear prophecies were made of better things to come in the Christian church. Herein also Solomon's temple was built, and various new and more glorious types of Christ were made evident than were in the tabernacle. To the degree that this temple of Solomon excelled over the tabernacle of Moses, and the cherubim, tables, altars, pillars, and all the manner of sacred instruments in the temple surpassed those that were in the tabernacle, so much more did God's goodness in this day exceed the goodness of former days.

The fifth day was from Israel's going into captivity to Christ's ascension into heaven. This day, for the greatest part thereof, was indeed a dismal day. Yet the delivering of Israel out of the Babylonian captivity was a clearer and fuller type of our redemption by Christ than any former deliverance. Whereupon this day it is said, "It shall no more be said, The Lord lives that brought the children of Israel up out of the land of Egypt: but the Lord lives that brought up the children of Israel from the lands of the North, and from all the land where he had driven them," (Jeremiah 16: 14-15). The re-edifying of the temple was also a principal type of Christ's resurrection. And of this temple it is said, "The glory of this latter house shall be greater than that of the former," (Haggai 2:9) so as these added much to the glory of this day.

But in that the Lord Christ was actually revealed in the evening of this day and all those prophecies were accomplished that were prefigured by the law and foretold by the ancient prophets, the goodness of God that manifested in this day far exceeded that which was in former days. In this respect it is said of John the Baptist, who saw and made known that promised Messiah, that he was the first that directly pointed him out, saying, "Behold the Lamb of God," (John 1:29, 36). Of him it is said, "among them that are born of women, there has not risen a greater," (Matthew 11:11). This was the surpassing glory of the fifth day.

The sixth was from Christ's ascension to heaven to his second coming unto judgment. This is the day of the clear and full revelation of all the glorious mysteries that were hidden from the beginning of the world till then. This is the day by which all the aforementioned new things and better things were conferred upon the Christian Church. In this day, as better things shall not be given, so better things cannot be expected while the world lasts. This is the day whereof we may say, "This is the day which the Lord hath made: we will rejoice and be glad in it," (Psalm 118:24).

In this way, from this exemplification of the increase of God's goodness in the several ages of the world, we may well infer that, "God has provided better things for the latter times."

Without question, God orders his good providence upon just and weighty reasons,[61] and though his counsel is unsearchable and his ways past finding out, in regard to the full latitude of them, yet has he left some footsteps wherein and by which we may observe some grounds of his wise proceedings therein. Among others, I suppose, these may be some.

Firstly, that the extent of his goodness may be more distinctly considered, more closely discerned, and more transcendently admired.[62] God's governing of his Church in the world by his providence is ordered in such a manner as his prudence in creating the world was manifested.

In that first great work, he still put off the better things to the latter days. He could, if it had pleased him, have created all things that he did create at once.[63] Had

---

[61] Reasons of God's increasing goodness.
[62] 1. The extent of goodness better discerned.
[63] God's works better and better.

he at once said, "Let there be light, firmament, waters, earth, all manner of trees, and herbs bearing seed, sun, moon and stars, fowls, fishes, beasts and man," they would all have instantly been. But voluntarily and purposely he took six days to create them, and in each day made several and distinct creatures, but ever the better, for the reason before specified. This will evidently appear by an induction of particulars, which follow in order.

The light which he created on the first day was indeed a glorious creature.[64] But either it was the element of fire (for nowhere else do we read of him creating fire) or else it was some other light, which was of use but for three days. For in the fourth day those lights were made, which have since continued, and shall continue to the world's end. So, either this light was annihilated when those were made, or else it was incorporated into the body of the sun.

The second day the firmament, or the atmosphere, was made and called heaven. Then also were the seas and dry ground made.[65] (Genesis 1:10.) These three – air, water, earth – are three elements from

---

[64] The first day's work.
[65] The second day's work.

which all bodies are made. These are more excellent than the aforementioned light, in regard to their continual use.

On the third day all the grass and herb-yielding seed, and the tree yielding fruit after its kind were made.[66] These vegetables, by reason of the life that is in them, excelled the former.

On the fourth day the host of heaven was made.[67] This day's work in the glory and immutability of it, and in terms of its constant perpetual motion, running most swiftly round about the world every day without wasting or weariness, excelled all that went before.

On the fifth day all the fowl of heaven and fish in the sea were created.[68] These having life and sense in them, and voluntarily moving from place to place, surpassed the very host of heaven.

On the sixth day, besides other creatures living on the earth, man was made in the image of God.[69] This was God's masterpiece and was reserved until the last working day. By this distinct increase of God's goodness, God is all the more admired and his wisdom, power, and

---

[66] The third day's work.
[67] The fourth day's work.
[68] the fifth day's work.
[69] The sixth day's work.

other excellencies all the better discerned. The like course therefore God took in his providence.

God provides better things for the latter times, to make those better things to be more earnestly desired and longed for before they come: and to be more highly prized and better esteemed after they're exhibited.[70] It is said, "that many prophets and righteous men desired to see and hear the things which were seen and heard in Christ's day," (Matthew 13:17) which were the last days. It is also said that the prophets, "searched diligently, what or what manner of time the spirit of Christ which was in them did signify, when it testified beforehand the sufferings of Christ, and the glory that should follow," (1 Peter 1:11). Certainly, putting off the great blessing of the exhibition of Christ to the latter times made it more desired and better esteemed. When he was exhibited, the angel that brought the first tidings thus expressed it, "Behold, I bring you good tidings of great joy, which shall be to all people," (Luke 2:10). And the blessed virgin, as soon as she conceived him in her womb, breaks out, "My soul doth magnify the Lord, and my spirit hath rejoiced in God my Savior," (Luke 1:46, 47). And good old Zachariah, when the forerunner of Christ was born, in

---

[70] 2. Better things delayed, making them more desired and esteemed.

great joy declares, "Blessed be the Lord God of Israel," (Luke 1:68). And another good old man, having embraced Christ when he was but a little infant, sweetly sings forth this swan-like song, "Lord, now let thy servant depart in peace, for mine eyes have seen thy salvation," (Luke 2:29). Their long expectation of Christ thus affected them, when at length their longing was satisfied.

God delayed his best to the last times, because in his unsearchable wisdom he ordained that his Son should be sent into the world in the latter age[71] that he might be known to be the best of God's gifts and to excel all other gifts that were before conferred upon the Church. He is said to be, "sent forth when the fullness of time was come," (Galatians 4:4). The church had been as a breeding woman. She began first to conceive when God made the promise of the woman's seed (Genesis 3:15). She grew bigger and bigger through many other promises, prophecies, types, and figures, by which her hope in the Messiah was nourished. At the fullness of time, she travailed and brought forth this long expected male-child. The better things, which were now brought to pass in this fullness of time, added much to the honor

---

[71] 3. Best things put off to the last days for Christ's honor.

of him that was then born: then was the fullness of God's grace and goodness manifested. This God ordered to honor his Son.

Up to this point I have addressed the doctrinal part of my text. It is now time to come to address its application. The uses of God's providence in reserving better things to the latter times are of both manifold and singular use. For[72] it affords a demonstration of the detestable nature of the Roman religion, which has directly perverted the aforementioned course of God's providence to his Church. For where God provides better for the latter times, they make these latter times the *worst*.[73] As they handle the matter, their Church under the gospel is in many ways in a worse place than the state of the Church was under the law. Among many other instances I will note only four.

Firstly, their public reading of God's Word, administering the sacraments, praying, and performing other divine services in an unknown tongue, make the mysteries of the gospel less intelligible, more obscure, and in every way less edifying than all other rites, types,

---

[72] Uses of God's increasing goodness.
[73] 1. Popery makes the last days worse.

and shadows under the law.[74] "Except your words are easy to be understood, how shall anyone know what is spoken? For you shall speak into the air," says the apostle. And again, "If I know not the meaning of a voice, I shall be unto him that speaks a barbarian, and he that speaks shall be a barbarian to me," (1 Corinthians 14).

Their unbloody sacrifice of a feigned transubstantiated body is far worse than if they had such sacrifices of beasts and fowls as were done under the law.[75] Those sacrifices at that time set out the virtue of Christ's death and nourished their faith and hope in the benefits thereof.[76] But the aforementioned popish sacrifice takes away the virtue and efficacy of Christ's sacrifice, if it could be taken away. For I demand to know whether the sacrifice they pretend to offer up is the very same that Christ himself offered upon the cross. If they answer yes, it is the same, there is no need to offer it up again. Was not Christ's initial offering sufficient? The apostle assures us that Christ's sacrifice on the cross is exclusively to be taken as a once for all offering, not to be reiterated. And if theirs is intended to be another

---

[74] 1. An unknown tongue less understood than types. Bellarm. *de effect Sacr.* 1.2.6.31 Rhem Annot. *on 1 Cor. 14.*
[75] Popish sacrifice worse than legal.
[76] Council. *Trid. Decret* 10. C.2. Bellar. *De Miss.* 1.1. C.5 et 12 et 1.2. C.7.

sacrifice, then the sacrifice of Christ was not perfect. For hereby the apostle proves the priesthood of the law to be imperfect; because another was to succeed to fulfill that gap. Some may say their offering up of the body of Christ is meant to be purely by way of application. However, that seems to contradict their own position; for they teach that the aforementioned transubstantiated body, offered up by a priest, is a true, real, propitiatory sacrifice for the quick and dead (Hebrews 7:27, 9:26-28, 10:10, 7:11). Further, the continual application of Christ's one sacrifice is the end of Christ's intercession. And yet they think to evade all these absurdities by a distinction between a bloody and unbloody sacrifice, saying that the sacrifice which Christ himself offered up was a bloody sacrifice, but that which they offer up, unbloody. To this distinction I answer.

First, it is without any warrant or ground from Scripture.

Secondly, being applied according to their position to one and the same thing (for they say that the body of Christ which their priest offers up is the very same that Christ offered upon the cross), this implies contradictory terms namely, that the same thing could be both bloody and unbloody.

And yet, according to their own position, their sacrifice cannot be unbloody; for they hold that the wine is transubstantiated into blood, as well as the bread into body, and both make one sacrifice. How can that be unbloody which consists of blood? And even more so, of blood poured out, as their wine is poured into a chalice, and out of the chalice into the priest's mouth.

Further, if it is unbloody, it has no virtue for the taking away of sin: For, "without the shedding of blood there is no remission," (Hebrews 9:22).

The third instance of their making the state of the Christian Church worse than that of the Jewish state is their unwarrantable and inhumane penance and other barbarous practices where they persuade men upon pretense of merit and perfection.[77]

The last instance that I will give of putting a heavier yoke upon the necks of Christians,[78] than the law did upon the Jews shall be the innumerable, unwarrantable, and intolerable rites which they impose upon their people. Such popish rites are neither instituted of God, nor have any warrantable significance

---

[77] 3. Popish penance more heavy than legal.
[78] 4. Popish ceremonies more burdensome than legal.

for those who use them, whereas the rites of the law had both their institution and significance from God.

Further, if the doers of said rites should plead them before God, what other answer could they receive but this, "Who has required this of your hand?" (Isaiah 1:12) or "In vain they worship me," (Matthew 15:19).

Much more might be said in manifesting the wrong and the blindness of those that allow themselves to be led with such blind guides. Blessed be God that has delivered us out of that Egyptian darkness.

The progress of God's providence unto the better gives us enlightenment into their folly of admiring such external types of Christ under the law as candlesticks, lavers, priestly vestments, and other such vessels and instruments of pure and fine brass, silver, gold, fine linen, silk, scarlet, pearls, precious stones and other materials glorious to the sight. They demonstrate their folly in that they do not understand nor discern the excellency of those spiritual and celestial things which God has now provided for his Church. Rather, we realize that those external and earthly, though seemingly glorious types, were mere shadows and figures.

Others, which we may call Jewish Christians,[79] may not adhere to these types of rites and rituals, but still hold to the Jewish law of former times in terms of what fish, fowl, and beast they still believe to be unlawful to eat. And yet God has forbidden us to call that unclean which he has cleansed (Acts 10:15), and reckons abstaining from meats, which God has created to be received, among doctrines of devils (1 Timothy 4:1-3). The last day also of the week they, still keep for their Sabbath, though the first day of the week, in memory of Christ's resurrection, is the day that is expressly declared in the New Testament for Christians' holy assembling together (Acts 20:7; 1 Cor. 16:15).

The progress of God's providence to the better is a great aggravation to the ungracious and ungrateful disposition of many people, if not of most, whom God has reserved to these latter times.[80] God has graciously done better for them, and yet they deal worse with God. Such are:

Those who remain blind and ignorant under the clear light of the gospel.[81] How can there be so little knowledge where there is such plentiful means of

---
[79] Jewish Christians.
[80] 4. Aggravation of gospel sins.
[81] Gospel sins. 1. Ignorance.

knowledge. Note the apostle's pronouncement for such, "If our gospel is hid, it is hid to them that are lost, whose eyes the God of the world hath blinded," (2 Corinthians 4:4).

Those who are unstable and carried about with every wind of doctrine, notwithstanding the evident demonstration of the truth now made known to us.[82] The apostle compares them to children, when for the time, "we ought to be as grown strong men," (Ephesians 4:14 and Hebrews 5:12).

Those who are ever weak in faith, full of doubts and fears (James 1:6, 7).[83] Christ often instructs his disciples in this (Matthew 8:26). Further, witness that catalogue of believers which the apostle references in Hebrews 11, that great Hall of Faith.

Those who take advantage, from the abundance of God's mercy, to exceed in sin.[84] In the apostle's time, in terms of this gracious extent of grace to great sinners, "Where sin abounded grace did much more abound," some made this sinful and unjust inference to let us "continue in sin, that grace may abound." These make sin the proper procuring cause of God's grace which is in

---

[82] 2. Unsettledness.
[83] 3. Doubtings.
[84] 4. Abuse of grace.

every way free: only God takes occasion from the misery in which sin plunges man to extend mercy to him, and that abundance of sin may not hinder the current of his grace. Rather in such instances he causes it to abound. Besides, they who infer this unjust consequence apply that to future sins, which is spoken of sins past, and extend that to obstinate and impenitent sinners which is intended for those who groan under the burden of their sins.

Those who from the comfortable doctrine of election to salvation infer that they shall assuredly be saved while choosing to live however they will,[85] not considering that they who are ordained to the end are ordained to the means that bring them to that end (Ephesians 3:4).

Those from God's wisdom in bringing good out of evil take occasion to do evil under this pretense, that good may come.[86] The apostle declares this judgment upon them, "whose damnation is just," (Romans 3:8), implying that damnation is their due, and that most justly.

---

[85] 5. Perverting election.
[86] 6. Doing evil on pretense of good.

Those who presume upon God's pardoning a sinner whenever he repents by delaying their repentance,[87] not considering that men do not possess the power to repent when they will. Those who do so may never repent and therefore never be pardoned.

Those who from that liberty by which Christ has made us free (Galatians 3:10) imagine that they are freed from *all* obedience to the moral law. Rather that liberty is only from the rigor of the law which binds us to a perfect fulfilling of it in every part, point and degree of it (Romans 13:10), and from the curse of it (Romans 8:1).

Those who deny the morality of the Christian Sabbath and profane it with all manner of sports, because the former day is changed by virtue of Christ's resurrection.[88] All these and others like them, "turn the grace of God into lasciviousness," that is, into all kinds of immoral living. The apostle gives this verdict of them, "They were of old ordained to condemnation," (Jude 1:4).

Those who, "having escaped the pollutions of the world, through the knowledge of the Lord and Savior Jesus Christ, are again entangled therein, and overcome," (2 Peter 2:20) and "willingly sin, after they have received

---

[87] 7. Delay of repentance.
[88] Profaning the Sabbath.

the knowledge of truth," (Hebrews 10:26).[89] In a word, all apostates from the true faith who deal most ungraciously and ungratefully with God. I may well use Moses' approbation against them, "Do ye thus requite the Lord, oh foolish people and unwise?" (Deuteronomy 31:6). Such as these grieve the good spirit of God, and they that commit such errors go far, "in treading underfoot the Son of God and counting the blood of the covenant wherewith they were sanctified an unholy thing," (Hebrews 10:29). By means of grace they were, "exalted unto heaven." But by their abuse thereof they are, "brought down unto hell," (Matthew 11:21, *etc.*). The inference which the apostle makes upon those who sin against the gospel is this, "He that despised Moses' law dies without mercy. Of how much sorer punishment, suppose ye, shall he be thought worthy, who has trodden underfoot the Son of God?" (Hebrews 10:28-29).

At the same time, much consolation may be gathered by faithful ones from the continual increase of God's providence in such sad, doubtful, dangerous days as these our days are.[90] For we may with confidence

---

[89] 10. Apostasy.
[90] 5. God's reserving better things to latter times makes us expect better in bad.

expect better things. The days wherein the prophet first uttered this prophecy were worse days than ours are; and to comfort the faithful that then lived, and those others who from age to age live after them, he revealed this promise.

There are more particular promises concerning a future glory of the Christian Church set down by the prophets in the Old Testament, and by Christ and his apostles in the new, especially in the book of the Revelation, than we have either heard of or seen in our days to be accomplished. The glorious city described in Revelation 21:10 and following is by many judicious divines taken to be a type of a spiritual, glorious estate of the Church of Christ under the gospel yet to come. I will not proceed to discuss this in particular, but what I do know for certain is that there are better things to come than have been since the first calling of the Gentiles. Among those better things to come, "the recalling of the Jews,"[91] is most clearly and plentifully foretold by the prophets.

But if any shall question this and other prophecies of the ancient prophets, the apostle Paul has expressly foretold a recalling of the Jews as, "a bringing

---

[91] The Jews to be recalled.

in of the fullness of the Gentiles." Some particular expressions of his in the 11th chapter to the Romans include these:

Verse 11. Having propounded this question concerning the Jews, "Have they stumbled, that they should fall?" (namely, totally and finally, never to be raised again). He gives this answer, "God forbid." By which he implies that they shall be raised again, that is, they shall be made a visible Church of Christ, and submit themselves to his ordinances.

Verse 12. This supposition, "If the fall of them be riches of the world, and the diminishing of them the riches of the Gentiles, how much more their fullness?" By their fullness, he means gathering them into the Church of Christ consisting of Gentiles, and thereby making that church full, when both Gentiles and Jews shall be joined together.

Verse 15. This question, "What shall the receiving of them be but life from the dead?" takes for granted that they shall be received and taken into the Church of Christ, and that this restoration of theirs will be as a glorious new resurrection.

Verse 23. It is said, "They also shall be grafted in," namely, into the body of the Christian Church. And further proof of this is taken from God's omnipotence, "For God is able to graft them in again."

Verse 24. This emphatic interrogation, "How much more shall these, which are the natural branches, be grafted into their own olive tree?" removes from all question that the Jews shall again be joined to the true Church, which is the olive tree here intended.

Verse 25. This restrictive particle, "blindness *in part* is happened unto Israel," shows that they shall not be finally blinded, but that at length they shall come to have their eyes opened, as they shall know and believe in Jesus Christ. This is further manifested by expressing the period of this limitation, thus, "until the fullness of the Gentiles become in."

Verse 26. This general phrase; "All Israel shall be saved," shows that there is a time to come when not only two or three, or a few Jews here and there throughout the Christian Church (as have been in all ages thereof) shall be saved, but rather that the whole nation shall be called.

Verse 31. This phrase, "Through your mercy they also may obtain mercy;" shows that God purposely allowed them sometime to abide in unbelief, that when they should be brought to believe, this grace and honor might appear to arise from God's mere mercy and free grace. The words in the text that follows show as much, "For God hath concluded them all in unbelief, that he might have mercy upon all."

In this way we see that there is a calling of the Jews to come, and that their calling shall be as a resurrection from the dead, as an incision of many more branches into a glorious tree. It is made clear that this shall be a universal, conspicuous calling of a whole nation, wherein the freeness and greatness of God's grace and mercy shall be evidently manifested. At this time there shall also be a number of Gentiles brought in, as may well be called the, "fullness of the Gentiles," (verse 25). This certainly shall be a most glorious condition of the Christian Church yet to come. Therefore, God will yet do better things for us. In expectation of such we may comfort ourselves, though for a while thick clouds of troubles cover the face of the Church, eclipsing its glorious brightness.

God's reserving his better things to the latter times is a cause for much thankfulness.[92] Had we lived in ancient former times, and believed the promises of things exhibited in these times, how should we have

---

[92] 6. God's increasing goodness requites greater thankfulness.

inquired and searched for them? As the prophets did (2 Peter 1:10). How should we have desired to see them? As many prophets and kings did (Luke 10:24). How should we have rejoiced to see this day? As Abraham did (John 8:56). Now that we are reserved to live in this time, to hear, see, and enjoy these better things, should not our hearts be filled with praises and our mouths opened to utter the same? God has given those who live in these latter days a great gift. It is an unspeakable advantage and benefit, so shall God not have the praise thereof? True believers now have greater cause than old Zachariah had to sing and say, "Blessed be the Lord God of Israel, for he has visited and redeemed his people," (Luke 1:68). Yes, than old Simeon had to say, "Lord, now let thy servant depart in peace, for mine eyes have seen thy salvation," (Luke 2:29). These old men saw the sun rising in the gospel. We see it shining forth in the full brightness thereof. Should we not then be thankful, even for the times wherein we live?

Therefore, let us be found to walk worthy of this good providence of God, in reserving us to enjoy better things.[93] As exhorted in Scripture, "We charge you that you would walk worthy of God, who hath called you to

---

[93] 7. Worthy walking.

his kingdom and glory. We cease not to desire that you might walk worthy of the Lord unto all pleasing; I beseech ye that ye walk worthy of the vocation wherewith ye are called," (1 Thessalonians 2:11, Colossians 1:10, Ephesians 4:1).

This word translated "worthy" does not intend any merit but rather a congruence and correspondence to that which it refers. This is evident by that phrase which John the Baptist uses, where he exhorts his hearers to bring forth fruits, "worthy of repentance," (Matthew 3:8), which our last and best translators express as, "fruits meet for repentance." And in the margin thus, "fruits answerable to amendment of life."

This word "worthy" might also be translated, "fruits which deserve repentance," that is, such as are to be repented of. And what are those fruits? Surely evil, such as those whereof the apostle said, "What fruit had you then of those things, whereof you are now ashamed? For the end of those things is death," (Romans 6:21). A catalogue of such evil fruits is recorded in Galatians 5:19-21.

The idea is that when both man's inward disposition and outward conversion is answerable to God's gracious dispensation, it is referred to in Scripture as "a worthy walking." Hereby, therefore, it is intended that we who live in these latter times, and enjoy the better things which God has provided for his Church, should more abound in knowledge, be more strengthened in faith, be more established in hope, be more enlarged in our hearts with zeal of God's glory, be more conformable in our lives to his holy will, be more charitable to such as stand in need, be more diligent and faithful in employing and improving our talent, more patient under crosses, more ready and forward to suffer for the name of Christ, and to seal up our holy profession, even with our blood if we are called to do so. It is not enough for us to be, "followers of them, who through faith and patience inherit the promises," (Hebrews 6:12), but we must strive to outstrip them. As we have more means of grace, so we must more abound in the measure of all Christian graces. The aforementioned, "worthy walking" intends this much.

But some may say, is this possible? Can the best of us now come near to Abraham, other patriarchs and prophets, in knowledge, faith, patience and other like graces?[94]

---

[94] How Christians are to excel the ancient Jews.

I say that indeed some had the spirit in such an extraordinary manner and measure bestowed on them, as they might excel those who live under the gospel. But the comparison is not so much between person to person, as between body and body. So as the point intended is that God's people in these times should excel his people in those times.

Again, though in some particular extraordinary gifts and revelations some of them excelled, yet in a full and distinct knowledge of all the mysteries of the gospel and in other graces we may and ought to excel them.

If you were persuaded to the aforementioned "worthy walking," I will boldly set before you a direction by which you may be greatly helped thereunto.[95]

In general, it is this, that in every one of the aforementioned days of the great *week* of the world, you can observe those eminent persons recorded in the sacred Scripture and the most excellent graces for which they are commended. Thereby you may look to be inspired to press on toward a holy emulation.

To help you in this further, I will attempt to set before you (as the apostle does in Hebrews 11) some of the prime examples in each of those days.

---

[95] How Christian's walk worthy.

In the first day note especially Abel, Enos, and Enoch. Abel was obedient in that he offered sacrifices that were acceptable to God. Enos gathered assemblies together to worship God and frequented the same. Enoch in all that he did, kept his eye on God to approve himself to God (Genesis 4:4,26, 5:24, Hebrews 11:4).

In the second day observe Noah, Japheth, Shem, and Melchizedek. Noah shone as a bright light in a dark and wicked world. Japheth with his brother Shem, covered his father's infirmity. Melchizedek blessed God for Abram's victory and encouraged his soldiers (Genesis 6:9,11, 9:23, 14:18,20).

In the third day there are many examples, including three great patriarchs. These all with much patience passed through many trials, lived long, and died in the faith of those promises (Hebrews 11:13). Joseph in a wicked and idolatrous land kept his integrity (Genesis 42:18). Caleb was a man of an invincible spirit in God's cause (Numbers 14:24). Joshua also with his household would serve the Lord, though none else did (Joshua 24:15). How careful were the judges to draw the people from idolatry and to keep them close to God? (Judges 1:16, *etc.*) Ruth, after she had been instructed in the true religion, went from her own country alongside her poor mother-in-law to the true Church (Ruth 1:16).

In the fourth day we have excellent examples of singular governors as David, Solomon, Jehoshaphat, Hezekiah, Josiah and others, who made it their main end and put forth their utmost power to advance God's glory, settle and restore true religion and peace, and establish good for their people. In that day there were also multitudes of faithful prophets who held close to God's word and would not falsify it for fear or favor. Such were Elijah, Elisha, Micah, Isaiah, Jeremiah, *etc.*

In the fifth day there were worthy restorers and reformers of religion, builders up of the house of God, redressers of grievances in State, and preservers of God's people from wicked plots of their adversaries. Such were Zerubbabel, Jehoshua, Ezra, Nehemiah, Mordecai, Esther, *etc.*

In the beginning of the sixth day, there were faithful preachers of the gospel, zealous professors of the true faith, merciful and charitable brethren, constant and courageous martyrs.

These being reserved to the beginning of the last day, wherein the better things were exhibited, answerably carried themselves, and were in many respects better than such as lived before them.

Should not we then who live in the latter part of the last day (to which better things are reserved than in the former part) endeavor to be better than all the former? What a shame it is to us to be so ignorant, so superstitious, so doubtful, so fearful, so cold and backward to good, so impatient, so discontent, so worldly, so wicked, as many of us are? If the men of Nineveh and Queen of the South shall rise up in judgement against the Jews (Matthew 12: 41,42) who lived in Christ's time, much more shall such as lived either in the beginning of this last day, or in other days before it, rise up in judgment *of us*. I will conclude this point, and this study too, with that inference which the apostle makes on a similar ground with these words, "Wherefore seeing we also are compassed about with so great a cloud of witnesses, let us lay aside every weight, and the sin which doth so easily beset us, and let us run with patience the race that is set before us," (Hebrews 12:1).

FINIS

Other Works Published by Puritan Publications

Books with information on God's Providence:

Christ Commanding His Coronavirus to Covenant Breakers by C. Matthew McMahon

Christian Truths Necessary for Salvation by Nicholas Byfield (1579–1622)

Four Discoveries of Praise to God by Alexander Hume (1560-1609)

God is Our Refuge and Our Strength by George Gipps (n.d.)

God's Sovereignty Displayed by William Gearing (1625-1690)

God's Voice from His Throne of Glory by John Carter (d. 1655)

Joseph's Resolve and the Unreasonableness of Sinning Against God by C. Matthew McMahon

Sparks of Divine Glory: A Practical Study of the Attributes of God by C. Matthew McMahon

Other Works

The Efficiency of God's Grace in Bringing Gain-Saying Sinners to Christ by Simeon Ashe (d. 1662)

The Glorious Name of God the Lord of Hosts by Jeremiah Burroughs (1599-1646)

The Nature, Necessity and Character of True Repentance by Zachary Crofton (1626-1672)

The Sovereign Efficacy of Divine Providence by Urian Oakes (1631–1681)

The Two Wills of God Made Easy by C. Matthew McMahon

The Vision of the Wheels: A Treatise on the Providence of God by Matthew Mead (1630-1699)

The Great Mystery of God's Providence, and Other Works by George Gifford (1547-1620)

God's Afflicting Providence, and Other Works by Francis Roberts (1609-1675)

Christ's Compassion in Our Trials by John Durant (1620-1686)

www.ingramcontent.com/pod-product-compliance
Lightning Source LLC
Chambersburg PA
CBHW022128160426
43197CB00009B/1188